SOUTHLAND

Harald Hanemann

Happy Christmas, 1992
for
Sam & Elaine –
Love –
Gatra & Bill

SOUTHLAND

and other
Poems of the South

Harold Lawrence

Cherokee Publishing Company
Atlanta, Georgia
1992

Library of Congress Cataloging-in-Publication Data

Lawrence, Harold (Harold A.) (1945–   )
      Southland and other poems of the South / Harold Lawrence. -- 1st ed.
           p.   cm.
     ISBN: 0-87797-251-6 (trade paper) : $14.95
     1. Southern States -- Poetry.   I. Title
PS3562.A9125S6   1992
811'.54--dc20
                                          92-23375
                                              CIP

This book is printed on acid-free paper which conforms to the American National Standard Z39.48-1984 *Permanence of Paper for Printed Library Materials*. Paper that conforms to this standard's requirements for pH, alkaline reserve and freedom from groundwood is anticipated to last several hundred years without significant deterioration under normal library use and storage conditions. ∞

Manufactured in the United States of America

First Edition

ISBN: 0-87797-251-6

98 97 96 95 94 93 92   10 9 8 7 6 5 4 3 2 1

 **Cherokee Publishing Company**
P O Box 1730, Marietta, Ga 30061

Loss — the experience that keeps us human — is the theme of these pieces. I have written and rewritten them while driving in the car, remembering the events and the people in my life which are now lost; and seeing from the road signs and symbols of the South slip past and be gone forever. This has been my grief therapy for a way of life that many will never know or mourn.

TABLE OF CONTENTS

Introduction

A poem takes familiar words worn smooth by time and arranges them in surprising new ways; it slows them down, catching a particular moment that somehow with pleasure we recognize. Harold Lawrence's poems slow the vanishing South and give the startling pleasure of remembrance.

Someone objects, "I can't remember the South. I never knew it." It's not necessary. These poems start with the South, but they go deep to the universal: the natural, the technical-industrial, and the human, caught in-between. The opening poems, "Docheno" and "A Death in the Mill, " isolate a child in the midst of technology. Sad "yellow rubber wings" replace the childhood's flights and fancy. In "Grandfather and Me," nature nourishes the boy and the hunter; yet the hunter is "splashed with the blood of the maple leaves," for nature, too, ends in death. The poems are full of history and lore (with even historical footnotes that lock in, from a non-poetic angle, the importance and reality of these countless forgotten people). And they are also simply about time: nature's time ("Planting Time"), clock time (waiting for the monstrous iron horse of Docheno to come), and human time ("Remembered in the clutch of chill").

With remarkable diction and figuration and a keen knowledge of regional particulars ("Hogkiller"), the poems ring changes on their dominant themes. Sometimes nature and the mechanical confront directly: the spider in "Night Rider," the ugliness of "Road Meat." Or nature becomes an image for humanity set on edge by its own violent techniques ("Fire Ants"). Sometimes back-country laughter blows over a small farm, as in "The Depression Pig." Occasionally nature and dignity and cheap blindness focus on the same object – perhaps a brick ("The Taliaferro Homeplace") – and spill over into social consciousness ("Trouble at the Primary"). Over the entire collection drama, irony, and transiency raise the human question mark.

If the poems are read a few at a time, they begin to put together, element by element, a complex and haunting world-view that lingers, resonates, and touches the spirit. If the style is occasionally too intense, or the drama too magnetizing, the South approves. Nor do the poems ever let go the power of undertone. Harold Lawrence has offered us a singular gift.

William Mallard
Emory University

Docheno

The little girl lies awake
in the late-night darkness
that has filled a rambling house
near a sidetrack of the Southern Railway
waiting there with the pops and cracks
of cooling tin
and the loud agony of nails crying out
in the clapboards
for that long low moan to reach her
from the hot wet maw of night.

She listens
knowing it will come
and hurl its distant fury into her room
shaking the bed and windows
and flashing its cold yellow eye
across the beaded ceiling
before reaching out to touch her
like a finger on the hand of death.

Bathed in the fear of many nights
on this one she rises
with the first premonition
clutching her gingham doll
and slips out past the unlatched screen
into the sultry warmth
of sweet shrub and honeysuckle
and into the outer dark
beyond the yard's edge.

No one sees the tender sacrifice
deliver herself up
in a fragrance of diesel and creosote
to the high gravel bed on the sidetrack

wearing her courage like a badge
and craning her neck to glimpse
the faint silver ribbons of the main line
on which the iron-shod monster will come.

She waits
for the rail under her bare feet to tingle
before placing her doll between the ties
of the moon-touched spur
and stepping back
to watch it take her place
in the risks and sanctions
of the imagination.

Out of the south the destroyer roars
its demon eye roving, searching for her
intent on devouring
the resolve in her marrow
with its wails and shrieks.
Pitching
and thundering like a black metal bull
on frenzied midnight rampage
it streaks past the last milepost
and catches everything in its gaze
looming in a bright and frozen instant
over one so small and vulnerable
ringed with a halo of maternal defiance
weak and buffeted in its wind
but unafraid.

Docheno: (pronounced Doh-shee-na). This sidetrack is located in the southeastern corner of Anderson County, SC, between the towns of Belton and Honea Path on U.S. Highway 178. From about 1914-1930 it was a busy shopping point for cotton, corn, grain, pulpwood and fertilizer. Local farmer and politician, Josh Ashley, was responsible for getting this spur of the Southern Railroad by his efforts in the SC Legislature. It died with the death of the railroad. It is said that the owner of the property where the right-of-way was granted, a man named Ben Cobb, opposed the sidetrack and was determined to prevent it from being built. He took a gun and a gallon of liquor and lay in the woods near the site, waiting for the construction crew to show their faces. It is said that by the time he sobered up, the track had been built, the crew had gone, and the line was in full use.

Grandfather And Me

At the first chill
a stillness comes to the fence-locked land
and the sanctity of the brush piles.
No shiver in the barbed wire
or stirring among the dried stalks
can touch the widening solitude.
Quiet settles
in the maze of mice-rattled fields
and in dead forgotten rows
like a faded memory of the man
who breathed upon this emptiness
and gave the land its life.

Remembered at the first chill
a wide-eyed boy who watched the woods
where the hunter entered and walked
splashed with the blood of maple leaves
and returned alive and smiling
dogs at his heels
and the forest red on his coat-sleeves
through fresh green graves of barley
and the rattling bones of dry cornfields.

Remembered in the clutch of chill
a youth keeping pace
in the white veils of boot-marked frost
as the hunter pushed his lagging dogs
beyond the range of eye and gun
with deeper and colder penetrations
on toe-frozen mornings
and blue-fingered afternoons
bending and catching on countless fences
until the light faded.

Remembered
in the land where night settles
in the brittle fields
and in old tracks on the frozen road
a man on whom the hunter leaned
as he burned for breath
wracked and winded from the empty air
the sun gone from his face
and the clamor dead
along the mud-scuffed banks
on that long slow walk back to the truck
and the squirrels barking
a last farewell.

A Death In The Mill

Standing on a ladder in the air-wash room
in a yellow rain suit
doing his best to fill the rubber boots
of a man
the boy hoses down the screens
washing to the floor
each moth-like particle of lint
the pressure of the trust placed upon him
equivalent to the pressure of the hose.
Alone on the top step
fearful for his balance
he breathes the stench of soured cotton
like a fragrance set aside for those
who are chosen for the solitude
of this chamber.

Like fluff from the waste-room
he has arrived here
by blowing out the ventilation ducts
and scouring down the brackish walls
in the groaning bowels of the mill;
by sopping up the oil and muck
under the hum and throb of air compressors
on holidays and weekends
when all things taste the same.

Above the shuttles and bobbins
he has risen in his own estimation
and navigated near the ceilings
on the dizzy heights of the beam racks
in the slasher room
taking risks disproportionate to the tasks

to reach this euphoric stretch
of tropical vapor
over the wet cement.

Pulling back his hood
to gain peripheral vision as he shifts
to the next set of screens
as commanding as a captain at the helm
he feels the slip of arrogance too late
and, like a victim coming from a coma,
abandons the false security of the hose
and stretches out on yellow rubber wings
to find that spot on the distant floor
where for a generation
those aspiring to his status
will point and emphasize to one another
how easily necks get broken.

The Next Best Thing To Christmas

We would look for him each summer
through those heat waves rising off the asphalt
hoping to see that broad bearded face
gleam at us
bringing with it the glories of the road
and dust from a thousand places
and that look in the eyes
that blessed little children
and invited them to touch
his kinship with them.

And then the word would come
from as far away as Elberton
that the Goat Man was headed east
on Highway 72
like a familiar soul in transit
stopping traffic in both directions
as he smiled and jingled
on his way to the river bridge.

The next day as we watched in earnest
knowing that he had stopped first in town
and at the Lone Oak service station
where he could always get
a junked tire to burn
we would behold his entourage
coming through the shimmering heat
down by the funeral home
streaming a comet's tail
of children on bicycles
caught in gales of red-faced mirth
wobbling and glittering behind him.

Suddenly he was there before us
barefoot in a railroad cap and overalls
smelling to high heaven
and carrying a little switch
more out of habit than in threat —
that God-like countenance resting on us
until we felt its goodness in our marrow.
Tying up in the shade of the water oak
bells tingling on his wagon
he'd introduce his goats to us by name
before going into the store
to pass out Bible tracts and try to sell
picture postcards of himself
which no one bought.

He never lingered at our place
longer than it took to down a yaller dope
and give his pets a sip or two
but would head out into those dancing waves
that seemed to split his body at a distance
until he was swallowed up by the hills
yet the thought of him stayed with us
on those summer nights back in the fifties
as grownups talked out on the porch
about his being a mythical traveler
of life's highways
bound for better worlds
and brighter days.

After the years had rolled away
like the wheels of that goat wagon
and his memory lay in cool quiescence
for the next twenty
I glimpsed him on the side of Highway 80
just outside of Jeffersonville
along with some forgotten part of me
and turned the car around
surprised to find him living
in the back of an old school bus
worn down and alone and broken-hearted
since his goats had died.

Reaching in to touch the sacred links
of his journey and mine
I could sense he had no more blessings for me
and no memory to rescue the awkwardness
when I told him he had always been
the next best thing.

The Next Best Thing To Christmas: Charles McCartney (over 100 years of age and alive at the time of this writing, 1992, in the Eastview Nursing Home in Macon, GA) was a legend throughout the South in the 1950's and 60's, known by the familiar name, "The Goat Man." In those days, he would travel the roads with a wagon and 35 goats, covering much of the United States, and living as he went among the people who allowed him to spend the night in their yards and on their property. During his travels, McCartney was based on property he owned near Jeffersonville, GA, erecting there at one time the Free Thinking Christian Mission and preaching regularly. He was known to all youngsters in the South as a kind and benevolent friend who always had time for them when he passed through their area. See: *The Macon Telegraph,* 12-30-1990, 1E, 8E.

Farm Home

Across the interstate
the emerging spring is apprehended
in a cameo of concentrated light
where an abandoned tenant house
with its sagging sheds and rusting tin
sits like an old squatter on the land
defining by its presence
the true rights of entitlement.

Out of the gray dead loins of earth
clover and chick-weed weave their brocades
over ancient chicken-yards and hog-lots
hiding for another season
the telltale signatures of refuse
and slaughter.

In the broken outline of fence rows
rising from a dormant strip
of briar and broom-sage
over-grown sprouts of plum bush and cherry
push their way to bloom and glory
shaming the ragged winter combs of sumac
and the burnt-out candelabras
of the old cottonwood.

This specialty
prepared like a salad in a golden bowl
evokes a forgotten taste of home
and a faint but undeniable hunger
from souls in exile on this road.

The Depression Pig

The Barron place has swapped hands many times
since that cold stark thin-ribbed evening
in the dearth of the Depression
when stars winked faint from privation
and the sole prized pig on a run-down farm
a gaunt and bony long-limbed Duroc
grunting hungrily and puffing hard
rooted too close to the edge
and fell into the dry well.

It plunged all those forty feet
squealing through tight muffled darkness
to splatter the black crusted bottom mud
and then rise numb and stumbling
to shake itself off and find
a narrow overhang to burrow under
and tremble against for warmth
while listening to the beating of its heart
pounding in its nose and ears.

When it did not come to his morning calls
and high-pitched shatterings
Bartow Barron looked high and low
peering first into that well
to find no signs of life inside
and then searching out his land
of red gullies and hedgerows
until he gave it up for lost
or hidden in a wrinkle of the night.

It was two weeks to the day
when he went over to the well again
and got down on his ragged knees
for one last desperate look
and staring at him from a gray-lit spot
through two narrow pits of gristle

were the sunk-back beady eyes
of that skinny thin-railed pig
shining like diamonds on a withered hand.

He threw down scraps and turnip tops
and lowered water in a foot-tub
while he studied how to save it
looking deep into the fire that night
after banking up the coals
and still seeing them through closed eyes
under cold covers
before stumbling upon the lame notion
of filling up the well with dirt
a shovel-full at the time
to raise the bottom to the top.

For the next twelve days
with sweat-stained clothes and blistered hands
he ditched and shovelled willfully
showering down on the protesting pig
and scarring the place with pot-holes
making such vain attempts
he would have given it up
had neighbors not pitched in with him
bending backs and scraping rocks
and hauling fill dirt from all sides.

Before that afternoon slipped quickly out
and the fall chill snapped the air
and crept along their sleeves and collars
tawny arms reached down and grabbed
mole-soft ears and upper joints
of an idea they had ridiculed
and with winks to that larger eye
that watches over its own
walked out Bartow Barron's winter meat.

The Depression Pig: This poem and two others, *Mule Talk* and *Double Take*, focus on a farmer named Bartow Barron, who owned acreage near Oconee, Washington County, GA. All three poems are based on true episodes. The pig story occurred in 1933, and while the house and farm are gone, the ruins of the dry well can be seen in the lanes of a pine plantation that now covers the property.

Tree Traffic

In streams of twos and threes
muscling up the sapling's trunk
life is on the march
as the frantic lines of the tent-caterpillar
lumber along
then suddenly balk and knot
in a three-pronged fork.

In a profundity of confusion
of rubbing and touching bristles
a mechanism activates
the nervousness of a biological clock
drowning a would-be riot
in wave after wave of webbing.

Further down the trunk
wobbling up and over
uneven crevices of bark
hundreds bump and shove their way
to closure in the clumsy ranks
urging themselves on through the sun-lit motes
in a blizzard of pollen.

Their soft frenzied columns
collect at every bend
like little wrinkles of mayhem
generating perpetual havoc
in their mutual transactions
while blundering ahead
through the wind-stirred chaff
of shimmering days.

Compelled and pushed along
in groping bumbling blindness
by others pressing close behind
they go from disgusting lowliness
to purpose
quelling in each fledgling movement
the first crude rumors
of flight.

Cleet

Even as a boy with a half-cracked smile
he loved to draw their oval shapes
and trace their images in breathed-on glass
but when he took out a pocket knife
and carved one in his eighth grade desk
and inked in the checkered shell so deep
its eternal visage could not be sanded out
Cleet became permanently affiliated with turtles
but could never really do them any good
until he got a driver's license
and drove the county school bus route
that took him on those country roads
where the majority of them crossed
inching along in their cumbersome body armor
like tired old warriors still on a quest
and he could stop the bus each time
during those early morning pick-ups
to move them out of the road
and always in the direction they were going
land terrapins, snappers and cooter-backs
all knowing the salvation of his touch
and thriving on his assistance
though it made him late so many times
he lost his route and sacred privilege
and had to give the keys
of that big yellow tortoise-shell bus
to some milk-fed freckled-face kid
in a blue corduroy Future Farmer's jacket
whose foremost aim and rush in life
was to feed and slaughter cows
and who didn't give a damn about turtles.
But it never fazed Cleet!
He'd move them when he could!

He had just picked up his seventh of the morning
out on the gravel road to Mineral Springs
and was cutting through to the main highway
behind the wheel of his father's straight-shift truck
used solely to haul trash out to the dump

but his to use on Saturdays
when he pulled over to pick up Sump
a Negro who worked at the lumber yard
and who was hitching a ride
but who did not know of Cleet's affinity
for the same lowly webbed-foot creatures
he'd been known to snag and stew
or else he would have walked.
When they turned onto the highway
about three miles from town
on the ridge above Mud Creek
Cleet saw one down in the flat
a big hooked-snout logger-head
probably disoriented by vibrations of the earth
with a hefty eighteen-wheeler further out
bearing down and closing fast.
There was no hesitation in him
as he surged the truck straight for it
knowing how the drivers of those big semi rigs
loved to try to flip them
by creasing the lip of the shell
with the edge of a tire
and catapulting them in an upward spiral
out as much as twenty feet.

Thinking to make the other driver swerve
Cleet headed for the center line
just as that semi's left front tire
converged on the black enameled disk
and would have died in a head-on
mesmerized by that oval shape
had Sump not hollered at him,
"What you doin', boy?"
and yanked back on the wheel
just as the airborne turtle
came shell-first through the windshield
like some strange alien craft
and landed in Sump's lap
and wet all over him.
After pulling over to the side
and picking glass out of their clothes
and examining the closed-up logger head

and guessing at its weight
and reflecting on how turtles touched a gentle side
and how it was a shame to kill them
they turned it loose down on the creek
and stayed until it waded out
and tunnelled in the bottom mud
Cleet proud to have saved it
yet apologetic about his mission
to Sump who thanked him for the ride
and walked on into town.

Broad River Woman

Old Annie Lou
squatting over in her garden on her stool
looking through the top part
of her fogged-up bifocals
fingers stained with blood
of the Johnson grass
absent-mindedly pulling up weeds
and going through the motions of a life
with nothing better left to do.

Old Annie Lou
with pantries full of jams and jellies
and a decade of snap beans
and a freezer packed
with once-delicious things —
who cannot give up the habit
of growing and gathering
and saving up for the hard times.

Old Annie Lou
dripping sweat at the elbows
unable to tell the time
by her husband's wristwatch
the humidity trapped in its yellowed crystal
like those old faded dreams of hers —
worn faithfully since that summer day
soft and unsuspecting
when she found him
face-down in the sweet corn
three rows over from
her right dirt-filled stocking.

Old Annie Lou
whose cracked churn and butter molds
are ornamental now
and whose calloused hands
grip hoe handles and hay forks
with a strength once admired
as lady-like —
fighting to keep
the only life she knows
and ignoring the changes
as long as morning comes
or until the ground no longer
recognizes her.

Walking John

Every morning in all weather without fail
he went to meet the train
sometimes wet below the knees
from blond dew-beaded roadside sage
and sometimes bent in a sweat-stained hat
on that same sacrificial return trip
feeling the holes in his pockets
and always without his boy.

He had put him on the train
brown-uniformed and waving
fodder for the howitzers of World War I
or some black-greased belt-fed machine gun
belching from a trench-worked copse
cross-threading the open fields
with its mesmerizing stitches
that sewed ranks fast in death.

He was there by the track in 1918
when the first of a thin brown stream
flowed from the cars
gas-sick and ghostly about the eyes
glad to be going home
and he was back to see the maimed
the last to come with bandages and stumps
and he was there again to meet the empty cars.

Every day for years he walked and stood
transfixed in the same insufferable spot
long after the official letter yellowed
and family consolation ceased
long after the steam trains changed to diesel
and brought home troops from two more wars
long past the time the lines switched to freight
and side-tracked their rusting passenger cars.

Last seen standing like a weathered sign
beside the cold gray sway-backed house
too old to make the trip
he would stare out at the road
as if to will a memory to life
and a form to step blithely
across the threshold of all mortal fears
and drop a worn brown duffle.

Planting Time

There are times of year
when life must exercise itself

when trees must bleed
and drip their precious fluids
in slow and sensual pulsations

when seas must thrash
blindly in their beds
responding to the advances
of a brazen moon

when air must stir
and carry on its soft winds
a fertile dust
to seed a yearning earth

when field hands must go gladly
into this great rhythm
and give themselves over
to its heat and exhaustion
bringing their hearts to bear
in tracing the ancient patterns.

Trouble At The Primary

The volunteers who ran the polls
signed him in with everybody else
but whispered conversations dropped
like stones thrown in a well
and splashed in quick succession
when he pulled the curtain back
and fed the ballot into the box
with those lean black fingers
as white as theirs on the underside
changing the world of a few who watched
idle and slack-jawed
as it rearranged itself
right there in the school gymnasium
forever deliberate and irrevocable.

Once outside the ordered lines
of smiles and decorated tables
the summer glare was not as harsh
as the men who ringed him
throwing punches timed by words and slurs
and buffeting him like children
in a friendly game of shove
the Chief's son taking out his wind
in a hail of pounding blows
so fierce and biting in the ribs
he never saw the knife
that sliced his stomach open
melting the surly faces to lumps
of nauseous and dispersing gray.

No one was left to cast aspersions
as he walked those solitary blocks
laced with aging oaks and boxwoods
bearing a faint brown and yellow tinge

and the first of autumn's ragged butterflies
to the door of the doctor's house
where he was refused and sent away
both hands clutched to his stomach
like one bent on dying
who could already see beyond the veil
and made to stand in the puddle
of his own helplessness
until someone driving by took pity
all the way to the county hospital.

The paper played it down
but word surged like electric current
through analogs of conversation
and federal agents came for weeks
to drift around and ask their questions
like the one he asked the Chief
when he had the first occasion
putting the query to him straight
about why he let his son
beat and reduce a man to helplessness
to which the Chief made quick reply
that Negroes had no business at the polls
and that anyone who came on ahead
got what was coming to him.

Before he left the Chief he said
that something bad would come of it
leaving the pronouncement to hang there
like a rancid joint of meat
by the main street store fronts
and he moved away to New York
while the Chief's son went off to war
to do distinguished service
and so the dark moment slept
long and deep and dreamless
in the psyche of the town
and on the bottom of page two
of the Abbeville Press & Banner
and it did not awaken.

Some things just have to lie and wait
like rabbits in a burrow
who want night to fall
or the scent on the air to change
and some things when picked up again
like old cold trails and blood trails
are never what they were
and thoughts of retribution have to scatter
as leaves do in a wind
before some things go full term
as this one did one April
when the Chief's son took his bride
of fifteen minutes over a blind hill
and straight on into the everlasting arms.

Trouble At The Primary: A Democratic Primary was held on August 24, 1948, in South Carolina following a 1947 court victory for Negroes guaranteeing them the right to vote in local elections. In the town of Calhoun Falls, Rev. Archie Ware, Negro pastor of nearby Springfield Baptist Church, came to the school gymnasium and was the first of his race ever to vote in that town. As he left the polls, he was assaulted and severely beaten and cut with a knife, though the county paper gave the incident very brief treatment. Ware recovered, moved from the community and never returned to live there. On 12-2-1991, Johnny Waller, pastor of the same Springfield Baptist Church, ran for Mayor of Calhoun Falls, SC, and won. See: *The Press & Banner & Abbeville Medium,* 8-26-1948, p. 2; *The Calhoun Falls News,* 12-4-1991, p. 1.

A Plea For The Last Town Oak

The old oak
with its stubby boughs and knobs
stands like a weathered relic
almost sorrowful and destitute
of leaves each spring.
Birds have long abandoned
its hollow places
and it has been more than a century
since children shagged up
to the limbs.

For what reason
did it become a sentinel
of the vanishing times?
Some would philosophize that its core
is wet and rotten
and deem its sawing and splitting
a waste of labor.
Old ones would swear against
failing memories
that it marks a forgotten corner
on a yellowed courthouse plat
but all agree
it has no place among us.

But if it could speak to us
and tell us of the knife-blades
broken off in its heart
or the initials that have healed over
or the generations of squirrels
that made their nests there
or the tales of idle men
who conversed in its shade
or the election notices

and theater bills tacked to it
there would be no hurry
to get it out of the way.

In all of the somethings
that must be done
in all of the progress
that must be made
in all of the usefulness
that has been out-lived
we pour contempt
on every little dying piece
of ourselves.

Neck

When he came home from work
that Friday before Christmas Eve
dust-covered
like he had slept for a thousand years
and found out that his neighbor
with the Spitz and the BMW
and different women on weekends
had filed a complaint with the city
about his Christmas lights
something in his mind switched off
so not even his wife could reach him.

After taking down the ones
lining the gutter and the ridge-row
and pulling others out of the shrubbery
and off the metal swing set
in heart-wrenching strokes
and uprooting from the lawn
through teared eyes
the plastic Santa Claus and manger scene
with vengeance swelling in his throat
he cleared out both nostrils
at the mailbox
in the customary way
then went next door
and, through teeth clenched with rage,
called out Mr. Yard-of-the-Month
and whipped his ass
all over the carport
despite the belly overhang
and a bad day hanging dry-wall.

There was more time this Christmas
from where he sat
bunched over at the shoulders
and in the same dusty clothes
to think about how it was
on that long-ago night
and how it was on this one —
locked up at three in the morning
in a cubicle of gray
away from decorations
and fireside revelry
and him without a spit-cup.

They had rushed him all at once
like an animal
without bothering to look
beneath that red-rimmed stare
to find the soft and sympathetic touch
who would spend a last dollar
on one more string of red ones
and who would fight
to bring a brighter season
and brief absolutions
to those apt to pass
and never once grudge
the electric bill.

It will not matter
what is done with him
or what ordinance gets passed
he will represent our collective interest
and put them up again next year
if no one else has the guts
and end up back here
to cast his familiar shadow
in this Herod's house
like an icon
that will always be with us.

Yens And Premonitions

Against white skies
birds string the wires
like notes on a song-sheet
and life passes
in a medley of varied scores
so bleak and unimaginative
that no one remembers the tunes.

Along the highway's widening scar
sutured in meadows of green and brown
wheels roll toward mystic vanishing points
and there is no returning
to innocent barefoot times
when the future was cradled
like a promised child
in the bosom of simple star-lit nights.

How silently the old order rearranges
and reluctant mentors casually depart
trust etched in their eyes
like cracks in old photographs
or time lines on wrinkled currency;
how silently the husks of their houses
and their ragged checkered fields
still reach in from the roadside
to touch new faces with their dreams.

There is no backward going
to the first fragile decade
graced by tangy smokehouse smells
on dark cool mid-days
or waftings of locust and persimmon beer
in a hallway churn
or that open-casket odor of wisteria

still blooming out there
in the old yards
as if there were no real ending.

What lies around the bend
of old roadbeds and rivers
and worn down terraces
scratched by Scovil hoes
are painful cheap deceptions
of everything abandoned and outgrown.
The future is become an orphan
that will beg its bread
from cold and cheerless throngs
and on nights far spent with grief
will cry out in restless sleep
begging to be remembered to the land.

The Peanut Man

You have seen him by the side of Georgia 20
or at a crossroads on Highway 29
looking back at you
like the old man and woman with the pitchfork
in the painting
poised to tell you something
about yourself.

The big black pot he stirs
and then covers with a sheet of tin
holds some of the promises of your childhood
which were never kept
and he still beckons with them
and he still waves.

Seated on a crate
or standing behind a board
lined with mountain cider and honey
he is the part of you
that can be found
right where it has always been
just like the tag
on his Red Camel overalls.

You do not ever have to stop
but if you will look for him
on the roads you take
he may just catch you
in those aging eyes of his
and offer you that taste of life
you have always wanted to keep in your mouth
and carry with you.

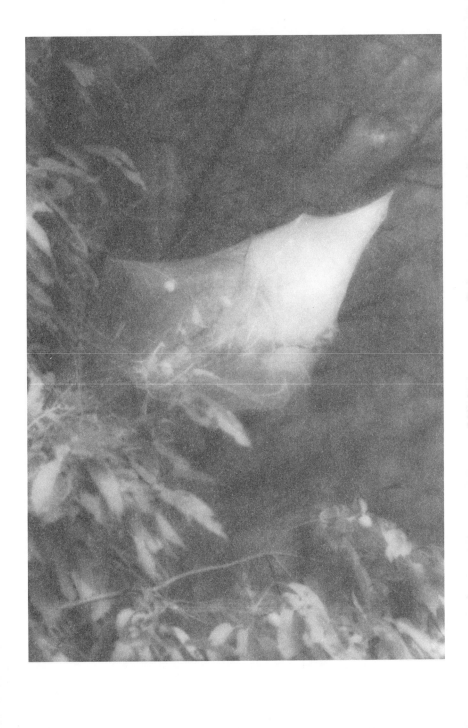

In The Long Canes

Who is left to mourn the loss
of the game that starved in the chestnut blight
or the moss-covered bones of the buffalo
that quaked from the panther's cry
on the swamps of the Savannah
or the vanishing of the passenger pigeon
whose clouds blotted out the sun
for a full half-day
and who is left to mourn these children
down in the Long Canes?

No one grieves for these
or knows the way to their common grave
deep in a lonesome woods
far from the lowest bird song
but there is grief to spare
for the tawny Cherokee
who rose up red and smiling
to hack and scalp their helpless forms
in that season of dreadful trial.

To the youngsters of that solitary train
making an encampment for the night
the howls and cries of death
wrung from the throats of relatives
and the screams of others carried off
struck such heart-felt terror
some hid their faces in the wagon bedding
to wait their bloody turn
while a few slipped off and hid
among the cold wet reeds
and whimpered at the noises of the night.

Mark well the lie that is buried
in the shallow grave of truth
about this land and its being bought
with such a price by our forbears
for in that frightened melancholy train
there was not one among them
who comprehended anything about a price
in the brassy taste of that blood-soaked evening
and not by their choosing was it paid.

If they could speak as one voice
and still be heard above the eloquence
of those who justify their slaughter
with glowing words about what it took
to tame that dense forsaken spot
still tangled in briars and reed canes
they would condemn each noble rendering
and take the time-honed lie
and bury it like a hatchet in our consciences.

In The Long Canes: On 2-1-1760, in the area of the Lower Long Canes of Abbeville District, SC, (now McCormick County), on a descent above Patterson's Bridge, wagons containing primarily women and children on their way to the safety of Augusta were attacked by Cherokee Indians. Of the fifty persons in the group, twenty-two were slain by the Indians and fourteen were carried away as captives. One of these, a little daughter of William Calhoun, was rescued some years later. After the Long Canes Massacre, as it came to be called, many children were found wandering in the woods. Fourteen of them were brought to Augusta, GA, some of whom had been cut with tomahawks and left for dead. Twenty of those massacred were later found by Patrick Calhoun and buried in a common grave where a marker stands as a witness to this grisly episode.

Road Meat

When a squirrel gets hit
on its way to a vaguely apprehended
elsewhere
it is understandable
or a rabbit after dark
paralyzed by the low-beam
or a dog chasing an erotic scent
who goes down before a glittering
of wheels
or toads by the thousands
seeking surface warmth after a rain
and getting waffled into the asphalt
or any other creature
for whom the lure of the road
is powerful
but a possum is different.

With soft bumbling body
and a nose for carrion of any kind
the possum takes to the road
to scavenge from its varied menu
and breathe upon these fallen
with a hiss and a grin.
Moving up and down the pavement
like a late-night hitcher
it hones in on easy curb-side kills
and checks out carnage at the center-line
dipping into shallow body cavities
or gnawing on a flattened bit of hair
and sinew
mesmerized in avarice.

Born to pilfer lumps of pink and gray
and leave its lump behind
it bristles from a rushing noise
and turns to defend its find
by snarling at the approaching danger
a stinking pudgy silhouette
as ugly as sin itself
illuminated for a second in the headlamps
like a target in the cross-hairs
never hearing the awful thump
and dying rank but game.

On The Cherokee Shoals

Ducks flew too high to shoot
on the Cherokee Shoals
but low and audible enough
to hear wing whistles
and glimpse their gleaming chevrons
shooting like silver bullets
through the morning fog.

Crouched in a mass of rock
in the shallows near the flood mark post
head thrown back and eyes shaded
by a damp right hand
I did not see them come
red-mouthed
and silent as corks bobbing
on the muddy Savannah
swimming it from the Georgia side.

Straining for ghost squadrons
in the roiling mists
how was I to know
the uninterrupted concentration
would prove fatal
as when sentries on duty
are garroted from behind?
Out of limp gray silence
I was distracted
saved by the low sobbing of a train
mournful and high up
on the trestle of the Seaboard Coastline.

Wild dogs! Nine of them
with wide delirious eyes
and laughing mouths!

On me before I could gain back
circulation in arms and legs
or stand to face them
stiff finger slipping all the while
for the little metal grid of the safety
independent from the rabbit fear
thumping through the rest of me.

I killed the closest three
the number two blue Peters
tearing through their grinning masks
leaving a red spray over the others.
And losing a boot in the muck
I shinned a bowed sapling on the bank
at the last nauseous second
hanging there as a marsupial clings
above the lunging and slavering
of its foes.

No barks or yelps accompanied
dripping tongues and rapid pants
and interchanging rows of flashing teeth
gone after a frenzy of plunging moments
sniffing and running silent
impatience like a glitter
in their yellow eyes
and on their lurid faces.

I saw them next nodding and wagging
in the dappled air
a half-mile downstream
where the river bent
in front of the sun's red yolk
burning through the vapors.

Swinging down on bones of porcelain
aged and stumbling
I laid hold of the gun
to break it down before reloading
and leave the plug
to moulder in their muddy tracks
before it could be the death of me.

The Man In The Box

The man in the box
is afraid to come out
and be seen for who he is
a painted head fastened to a spring
nodding and bending without a soul
a bobbing smile of pleasure and amusement
that moves to cranked-out music
until eyes and hands grow tired
and he must hang there motionless
or be stuffed back inside
to press his head against the latch
and wait for light and joy.

Millwood

Those who went there in the twenties
to picnic with their beaux
and walk about its silent grounds
running their fingers in the cool grooves
of the giant white millstone
and feeling the light tinder of the cork tree
had no inkling of the flair for genius
lavished on each terraced moss-covered step
and poured out upon the groves and arbors
forming a radius from the chimneyed ruins
in their trampling of the tea gardens and herb beds
and their eating of simple sandwiches
while idling away the time
and trailing slim bare feet
in the Savannah's muddy current
or wading out to see what fish sunned
in the rocks of its shallows.

Down in the crevices of the cellar bricks
and in the dried-out pith
of a long-dead fruit tree graft
and under the Savannah's glittering silt
where a single lead pipe corrodes
the marks of a man are loosely worn
like the rust in old dirt
that once was a nail
and his is not a lucid memory
in the town that bears his name
or in the final stand of muted oaks
offspring of his planting
that are the last lingering witnesses
to the lichen-flecked remains of his estate
along with scattered lightwood stumps
and a random molded chinquapin
embalmed by squirrels a century old.

How quickly human passions roll downstream
tumbling over time's incremental spillways
to that final place of distribution
where they break up on its black-rocked shoals
and how deliberately the outlines and imprints
made by a builder's hands and tools
are carefully reclaimed and overtaken
by hawthorne, vine and bramble
until the shards of every enterprise
lie scattered underneath a melting humus
so diffuse and safely hidden
that the soft-sculpture landscape
turns back into ordinary earth and sky
and the image of the creator
ripening in a few volunteer kernels
is borne off by the crows
as though it never was.

Millwood: James Edward Calhoun (1798 - 1889) returned from the Navy in the 1820's, bringing with him many exotic plants which he deposited on a 900 acre tract near the present town of Calhoun Falls, SC, called Millwood. Calhoun developed this property in the 1830's and became known as a remarkable but eccentric planter on the Savannah River. His favorite attire was white linen suits and wooden shoes which he sometimes wore in the winter. He ran a pipe under the Savannah to gain his drinking water from a spring in Elbert County, GA. Millwood, by the 1860's, produced great amounts of cotton, corn and other crops, with a slave population exceeding 200.

In the late 1830's Calhoun married a woman named Maria Simkins and was so in love with her that he built her a house on a knoll in the shape of a ship. A few years later when she died in childbirth along with her child, Calhoun never entered the house again and allowed it to rot to the ground. He became a recluse and remained on his plantation estate until his death, devastated by the death of his wife and child. See: Ernest M. Lander, Jr., *Tales of Calhoun Falls,* pp. 1-8.

41

Collectables

Grudge not the field mice
that tunnel through the hay bales
nor the crow that pulls up sprouted corn
nor the rabbit nor the deer
that graze the garden edge
with their incessant nibblings
and treat them not as worries
which gnaw their way through memory
and feed upon the contents
of silver sleep-touched dreams.

It is impossible to preserve
the season's yield intact
or to lay up in storehouses
the great harvests of the years
but if there is levity enough
in all the hailing forth
from hallowed farms and fields
there will be compassion
for those relentless creatures
scrambling for their tithe
and for the remnant
lost in the abundance.

Tattin'

Even with times set hard and the money gone
and being left to rock one's way to boredom
on a front-porch swing in the magnoliaed South
where all the land that Papa owned
got sold when it played out
to pay the taxes
there was still some saving grace
if a body knew how to tat
or that's what Isabella Simple thought
each time she'd sit on Tuesday afternoons
crocheting those little bootees
the way her mama taught her
and remembering how she always said
that most people who did handwork could not tat
out of an in-bred laziness
or thinking it too much of a pain
and eye-strain to fool with fine thread
but knowing, too, that Tuesday was a time
over at the Community House
when Colea Griswold and Camilla Butts
and Eugenia Singletary
met in the sewing room together
to tat and socialize
restricting membership to those genteel enough
to bring their tatting
and contribute to the finer things.

Not being one to covet
but wondering why she'd let herself
enjoy contentments of a lower plane
and miss out on life's higher compliments
Isabella flung the bootees down
and in a fit of righteous passion
dialed up her Aunt Jessie in Macon
and yelled in her good ear

until she promised to teach her how to tat
and would Sunday afternoon be soon enough
to come and fetch her to the house
and could she stay a week or so
and not run out of her medicine
or that special hand cream they did not carry
in the stores of Terrell County
and should she go ahead and buy
thread and a hand shuttle
or would Aunt Jessie bring some?
After laying to rest the questions
and dusting off the door facings
and fluffing the pillows in the guest room
and finding those embroidered pillow cases
her aunt had given her years ago
and pointing the ancient Dodge to Macon
like a long black arrow
Isabella hoped it was not too late in life
to feel she had finally arrived
and began to set her mind to it.

It was so hard she stuttered for two weeks
but finally learned to get a ring
and make her picots look the same
and tie a Josephine Knot
Aunt Jessie had to put under a glass
and look at extra close
to pronounce it certified
but the day she did a Hen and Biddie
sitting by Eugenia Singletary
there under the halo dryer
at the Beehive Beauty Salon
the culmination of her efforts
bore the fruit of a Tuesday invitation
and she drank in affirmation
like a blessing from heaven
and felt a vindication
that gave her back the place
her papa had ordained some years before
which Aunt Jessie would hear none of
on the trip back home
as she voiced a livid protest

about being hustled off to Macon
once Isabella learned to tat
and treated like goods and chattel
and with no regard as family
which Isabella could not hear
with her heart set on Tuesday.

The afternoon wore on at a snail's pace
as the minute hand dragged itself
up the face of the O.G. Regulator
toward three o'clock while Isabella sat
with a dry mouth and sweaty hands
staring at the what-not shelf
and coming instantly alive
when it chimed the three-quarter hour
snatching up her tatting basket
and barreling out of the driveway
like someone on the way to reckoning.
In the cool dark of the Community House
humming with wasps trapped in the ceiling
she opened the door to the sewing room
spoke to the ladies and took the place
Eugenia Singletary alluded to
with the sleight of her hand
feeling a great and singular reverence
and savoring its delicious taste
until Camilla Butts poured forth
a fusillade of coarse talk
to rend her ears
and tear her world asunder
leaving her so distraught and disgusted
that she got up and left
or that was the talk on Thursday next
down at the Beehive.

Deliverer

Perched on a naked limb
jutting out over frozen space
above the activity of a highway
a red-tailed hawk
poses like a specimen
in a taxidermist's window
reading the scenery
with its golden eye.

Poised near the creek
the odds are improved
despite the frost
clinging in the low places
and the absence of cover
for creatures who must come to water.

After a time
it detects a tremor in the air
and on the landscape
an inference of movement
below the dead grasses
and it rises
in gathering twilight
and builds its spiral
into an imaginary web
before falling like a thunderbolt
talons extended
on what has volunteered itself
as prey.

A brush with the ground
before shearing away
nets a squirming writhing mole
blind and terrified
prised from its dark sanctums
and borne up for a brief time
to rule at last
over all that it has known
and to feel in a rush of cold
the fright and the freedom
of wings.

Horace, The Wise

In the spring I would sit with him
after a day of plowing
and hear his stories about the boll weevil
and the Great Depression —
stories as good as the plug
of Full Bloom tobacco in his jaw
that gave off a whiff of fruitcake
when he would spit it out
into the old sand
of the clean-swept dirt yard.

In the late summer we would make our way
past aging cantaloupes and watermelons
corrupt and spewing
to a spot in the sorghum patch
where we would talk before stripping the cane
and he would fish in his pockets
for the pods
to show me the difference
in a Wade bean and a half-runner
at the end of the season.

Autumn found him staring from his porch
at the ragged quiet fields
like one of the ancients
whose time had come
or seeking the cherished but lowly companionship
out back by the hog lot
where purple poke weed grew in the fence
shelling the dried corn into a tin bucket
its echoes rattling like shot
against the empty afternoons.

He would spend clear winter mornings
with the doors and windows rolled up
in an old junked clouded blue Mercury
parked by the rusting Farmall
reading a yellowed Market Bulletin
like it was one of the classics
and feeling the warm light
reach in and touch his bones
and bless his thoughts
with graciousness.

When time moved everything along
and the old house was locked up and boarded
and the weeds and vines took the place
he sat out the final months
by a window
in the house of a city relative
waiting like an old philosopher
for a revelation that did not matter
and visiting the child within himself
who could still drink in the wonder.

Spring Is When

Spring is when
harrows are laid to the earth
like fingers on a hand
turning up the damp rich scent
of compelling odors
and rich musk
sparkling on the rigid tines.
In seasonal rhythm
they stroke winter stubble
until it is moist and yielding
and the compulsion to conquer
has been satisfied.

Sarriday

It's Sarriday
and out in front of the superette
an iced crate hits the sidewalk
like a lure on a smooth surface
causing ripples of interest
until it sits awhile
and the fish smell runs out with the melt
at the bottom corners
like silver lizards
racing one another to the curb.

On the third pass
a hand reaches down
and flips a mullet by the tail
until its dead glazed eye stares back
and the voice with it
recites a familiar verse:
"If I had a quarter
I'd get me one of them thangs."

It's Sarriday
and things are slow at the cafe
as the old man with red eyes
and a half-chewed tooth-pick
peels the hide from a yellow onion
and cuts it up like bait
and fries it on the grill
treating each cremated piece
with the reverence of a burnt offering
once it mingles
with the irresistible grease.

The pull of the exhaust fan
above the door
sends an aroma forth
like the dreaded smell
of plague stalking the streets
tantalizing into rebellion
children with hollow stomachs
who must go home
to their black-eyed peas for supper
or the eternal bowl
of corn-bread and clabbered milk.

It's Sarriday
with one hour left on the clock
in the town barber shop
where it is almost time to sweep up
what little hair there is
and the County News has been read
for the fourth time
and the fear of being white side-walled
still hangs in the room
as thick as talcum
on the slats of late sunlight
coming through the Venetian blinds.

There is still a twinge of forlorn hope
that someone will pass by
the little tray of penny candy
under the rusted electric pole
of never-ending red and white
and pause and take one
and come inside
trusting the possibility of nicks
and gaps
to the luck of the draw.

It's Sarriday
and while the streets roll up
the lights in the pool room come on
as the Kid chalks up another big one

running the tables with an eye
that never leaves the eight ball
the smoke from his butt
ringing him like a halo
and the ash almost touching
the peach fuzz on his chin.

Tonight he's laying odds
that he can hustle four out of five
if he wins at matching quarters
for the first break
and the solids roll to the corner pockets
and the cue banks to the right
and the fellow he is playing
is just some dumb son.

Black Tuesday

Into the dim-lit prison's maw
and down the silent corridors they came
these Knights of Mary Phagan
prepared to flush their quarry
as quickly as one would twist
a rabbit from a hollow tree
and take it quivering and warm
into firm determined hands
as they were taking Leo Frank
and stifle out its life.

Grasping arms and legs and hair
they twisted him off a hospital cot
and down to the front entrance
and out to the idling line of cars
nightshirt flapping its good riddance
while other prisoners whispered theirs
and word passed cell to cell
that a mob had forced the gates
and overpowered the late-night guards
and that Frank's time had surely come.

The northbound ride from Milledgeville
at times bare-kneed and pleading
from the backseat-floorboards
wore down each iron-bound resolve
like a cat eating a grindstone
and there was a momentary urge
to turn around and take him back
a few miles shy of Marietta
until morning streaks and kindled rage
ignited by the roadside and prevailed.

They hanged him from an obliging limb
pulling up the hemp and tying off
as the freshly sutured neck wound gaped
and the body writhed and kicked
its way to perfect peace
then swayed there in a light wind
softened by birdsongs in the woods
its spirit streaking off at once
ridden by the same night witch
as children who cry out in their sleep.

Black Tuesday: On the night of August 16, 1915, twenty-five men calling themselves the Knights of Mary Phagan forced their way into the state penitentiary at Milledgeville, GA, and abducted Leo M. Frank, a prisoner convicted of the 1913 murder of Mary Phagan in the Atlanta Pencil Factory. Frank's sentence of execution had recently been commuted, creating rage throughout Georgia and the South among citizens who were convinced of his guilt. After four weeks in prison, a fellow inmate attacked Frank with a butcher knife and cut his jugular. Miraculously, two other prisoners who were doctors clamped off the bleeding and sewed up the seven-inch slash in his throat. Frank was recovering from this attack when he was abducted and taken in a motorcade to Marietta, GA. He was hanged by this group about two miles from the city on Roswell Road. The Knights of Mary Phagan were resurrected later and reorganized into the 20th century equivalent of a 19th century vigilante group and took their name, the Ku Klux Klan. See: *Union Recorder,* Milledgeville, GA, 8-17-1915; Leonard Dinnerstein, *The Leo Frank Case,* UGA Press, 1987.

Haircut

They took his high-chair out in the yard
and sat him in it
and got a man up the road
who had done some barbering
to come and clip the curls
and handle the rage and violation
welling up inside.

Through streams of tears and mucous
he beheld in a shattering of light
the one who had come
silver gleaming in his hands
to change his world forever
with the flick of a wrist
and the flap of a home-made apron.

Shaking with disbelief
as tiny portions of himself
blew in all directions
he could not wipe his eyes
without the gossamer sticking
and each little breeze stifling
like the smile of the sympathetic thief
who stood over him
taking off a last inch of time.

After dusting talcum lightly over the fear
and returning the cold instruments
to the King Edward cigar box
strong hands uprooted him
and brought him for an instant only
face to face with the Spoiler
of his dreams
who lowered him differently
to anxious arms no longer large enough.

The Madstone

The open kitchen was thrown wide
to thick golden shafts and far-off notes
of black-yoked meadow larks
like a doorway into summer
the morning the dog came in
large and bold and in its prime
with eyes blazing and mouth spotting foam
and a sideways gait
which took it at a ragged canter
past two children at the table
to the woman standing by the basin.

The moment froze before its madness
but when that growling mouth
flashed against her ankle
the oldest sprang and knocked it off
with a stick of splintered stove-wood
only to have it turn and blur
and fasten upon his hand.
Like strangers in a dream
they drove it from the house and yard
and rang the bell on the post
before the sickening life-long fear
swelled in their wounds.

Both horses wheezed and trembled
wreathed by a throng in the fresh first-dark
as strong hands lifted from the wagon
an ashen mother and her child
and bore them like solemn sacred burdens
up the steps of the Harlem bank
where the vault door clicked and opened
as they blanched in the horse-hide chairs
and the town physician reached inside

like an aging Hippocrates
and lifted from its darkened pouch
the Gibson Madstone.

Hope glittered there in lamplight
when the famed marble-smooth deposit
retrieved from a deer's gall
was passed like a talisman
beneath wind-stirred flecks of desperation
churning in their eyes
and gleamed again when it was brought
like a wet worn creek stone
sleek and sucked
from its milk-white solution
ready to stick on the swollen cuts
and draw out the gray madness
and fall away when it could finally dry
and leave its peace.

Knowing there was one at home
still in the high-chair
and others running barefoot
who still looked and leaned to her
the bitten woman sealed her fate
against soft pleading and persuasion
insisting that the boy go first
and watching as the suction
pulled him back into her clutches
and waiting without sorrow
for the stone's renewal
and the morning application
to those throbbing bluish holes
already ebbing courage and constraint
at her ankle.

She suffered in the next two weeks
with sweats and chills and jerks
the violence in her eyes
setting her own teeth to grinding
until she could not bear for them
to look at her.
There toward the last

tied to the bed and crying helplessly
head flinging from side to side
they brought the stone that long way
and pressed it to her raging flesh
where it clung until she kicked it free
and trembled with the knowledge
that somewhere beyond its power
the true sign of salvation
was a mother's love.

The Madstone: The woman who died from the mad-dog bite was Tommie Elvirah Wheatley Blackmon (1860 - 1897) who married William Steven Blackmon, Wilkes County, GA. Of their nine children, the two in the story are Elijah ('Lige) and Jimmy. After the incident of the bite, mother and bitten son, Elijah, were carried to neighboring Columbia County to the town of Harlem. In the vault of the Harlem bank was kept the Gibson Madstone which was applied to the wound in the following manner: The stone was taken and placed into a milk-type liquid. It would then be adhesive when attached to human flesh. It would stay in position, supposedly drawing out the poison, until it dried and fell off the wound. The stone would need time to dry thoroughly before the next application. Elijah Blackmon lived until 1978. The wounds of the dog bite were still visible on his folded hands as he lay in the casket.

The Politics Of Flowers

With proud uplifted heads
Queen Anne's lace dots the fields
like the white bivouac tents of soldiers
from a story-book campaign
concealing in serenity
the mindless strife in nature
going on beneath their canopies.

Stunning in fresh dress whites
they stand in review
with the same practiced demeanor
sported on every other tour
bearing their vaunted pretensions
like smug marionettes on parade
who know the drill.

They appear much the same
as crowned heads of state
towering over lower common grasses
nodding their condescensions
in every lift of the wind
yet so tenuous in their government
that a puff of it provokes hysteria.

Among these bobbing parasols
where countenances alternate between
the regal and ridiculous
human frailties are portrayed
on wretched spindly stalks
as each, striving to show forth,
brushes against the other's fragile dreams.

Revisiting The Hide-Out

Under a treasure map of summer stars
the ragged profile of the rock's hard face
juts from the hillside
like an aged sentry
long abandoned by his detachment
yet found after all this time
still guarding the once-secret entrance.
On disputed darkened ground below
lost in the night shade
the heart of a rabbit thumps its wild rhythm
in softened muffled fur
scented but unseen by the orange eye
of a gliding fox.

Larger predators than this stalked here
where silent dim-lit decades
lying a corpse in briars and vines
betray no sign of the rude barricade
which checked a thousand onslaughts
by arch-fiends of the imagination
or the make-shift fort of lapped pine boughs
or the little cedar stump
that was the look-out.
These remnants of a covert universe
repeatedly touched and beloved
among the heart's symbols
now lie quietly about like a scattering
of bones.

This was a chosen spot where children
in communion with themselves
fought wars
and held their solitary rendezvous
in the days before their laughter

poured down the stream of the years
and out of hearing.

Nothing can be done to save these places
used for a time and then recycled
for the next cherished episodes
in nature's tenative arrangement.
The changes are stark and irrevocable
though slight to the mind's eye
where cliffs and fields and forbidden woods
will always be the size they were
to the fresh untiring souls
who now inhabit these aging frames.

As leaves and other residue collect
in the crevices of the windfall pines
as ragged seasons spin their dreams
like winding cloths
so will the instincts in us yearn
and strive to locate and reclaim
the unmarked graves of play
scanning the peripheries
of the remembered real
for that which is missing from
the center.

August Meeting

On the morning she got the call
she rose up from her pallet
by the white child
flat bare feet cushioned
on the wood shavings
and while smoke still curled
stole away past cooking fires
and oaks encircled by the tents
to a place in the arbor near the stand.

Kneeling there with palms upraised
giving the high sign
perspiration dripping from her elbows
and head thrown back in adoration
and eyes on the rafters
she called out, "Here am I!"
like when Samuel heard the voice.

When He spoke a second time
it was with pain
like a blade between her shoulders
coming from the depth of labored breath
love, mercy and grace coming with it
like a fire in her bosom
gripping the hand-smoothed altar rail
and crying out from her
"This world and one more!"

As the night sounds hushed
and the mist rose up
and gathered round her like a choir
she moaned once
and gave up her ghost
passing through the portal
with a quick backward glance
at the tired old sack
with wide sightless eyes
that lately beheld the sweet chariot.

Where will you tent tonight
Aunt Creasie?
Will it be in the bosom of Abraham
or at the feet of Jesus?
Will there really be angels
to watch over you
and will you get to hear
the music?

Winter Birds

Across gray skies
the flights of birds
bound on the currents
in dense black groups
suspended between moments
unrelated to all grounding
yet synchronized
and in rhythm
with the inner references
that hold them there.

They swerve
and dive and rise as one
instinctive consciousness
that cannot operate
in singular patterns.

They seem to mimic
in their flight
those who plunge and climb
the extremities of impulse
oblivious
to the gravitational pull
and indulgent
in the brief joy
of becoming one.

Hog Killer

If you don't hit it just right
in the center of that imaginary x
between the eyes and ears
if you miss because he moves
or if your shot is off
he is liable to get excited
and thrash about and bruise himself
and the blood will stay in the meat
and he won't drain properly
when his throat is cut
or so says Jerome
his words forming a circle of the owners
and him leaning against a store-room wall
as black as the shadow he is standing in.

From Land-race to Durocs
they have learned to listen to him
and note the differences
and watch him heat the scalding pots
and time the dipping of each end
so the hair won't stick
and make the cuts for the gambrel stick.
They have seen him take out the lights
and the "deef-ear"
with a reverence they will never feel
and clean the entrails by using the rhythm
of his fingers
like his daddy taught him.

There was a Hampshire way back
who got up after he was stuck
the knife still in him
up to the hilt
and he got among the others

and they smelled him and went wild
and commenced biting and kicking him
and rolling in his gout
so that no hand could come between them
and the owner's face went white
as rendered lard.

While he cursed
they dragged the dead one out
swollen and stiff by this time
blotching purple and blue all over
as they scraped him.
When they did all they knew to do
somebody called Jerome
known then as Mose's boy
and he came politely and told them
that it "won't no good killin' ground"
and spent the morning cutting out
what blood he could
and drawing out the rest with salt water
before chilling it
and grinding what he could save
in sausage.

Then he went out to the others
and settled them down
talking to them and wiping off the blood
where it had dried
and shoveling out the ground in the pen
that was tainted with it.
Then he felt their bruises
and rubbed them with something
of a spice smell
and they let him do it
like they were bred to it
and they were hanging on his hooks next morning
or so says Jerome.

State Of Grace

When they came in a box of waxed cardboard
with breathing holes large enough
to stick your fingers through
their peeping came out of the blackness
along with faint pecking and scratching
and that once-a-year odor
as sharp and penetrating as a herald
announcing colored Easter chicks.

The blue one sickened and died
its eyes concealed in slitted lids
the green one got mashed in the door screen
but the red one lived to be a pet
until it grew into a nuisance
with incessant runny droppings
in the most sanctified of places
and its gangly leghorn hunt and peck
that kept it constantly underfoot.

I feared for it the day
it was taken up by its feet
head arched out to right its world
and tossed into the chicken lot
red now only about the eyes
to cower in a corner of the wire
watching the larger buff Rhode Islands
with quiet sullen malice
and stalking as an outcast
among plump maternal barred rocks
prey to countless floggings
afraid and alone and unprotected
pecked bare by the roosters
and often hidden by their black-green plumes
until it won grudging acceptance.

On each first Sunday of the month
it was spared ax and chopping block
as one righteous in remembrance
watching its antagonists through octagon wire
as they flopped and bled
disgracing themselves in death
and leaving hideous examples
for the ones whose turn would surely come.

When the last yellow brood of yard chicks
was swallowed by a chicken snake
and the unproductive layers made their way
one by one to the dinner table
a gaunt white-feathered mendicant
with faint flecks of red about its eyes
enjoyed the solitude of the lot
and watched the moss encroach and heal
the fine-worn barren places
that the meek are destined to inherit.

Twister

He was not even from the place
yet the one time he allowed himself a night
of dark quiet restful hibernation
in a no-tell roadside motel
as nondescript as fill-dirt
and without the customary flashing light
he wound up tossed out here
with a numbing of the outer extremities
flat on his back in a field
a hundred yards from where his room had been
lying stone-like in wet sucking mud
that stuck to his neck like resin
and smelled like a fresh-dug grave.

Beyond him lay a clutter of wrecked souls
moaning in their broken heaps
and a dim white scattering of cement blocks
and stark ceramic toilet fixtures
protruding like fat uneven headstones
from the welts of ruptured stinking ground
bathed in distant bobbing beams
of flashlights bouncing back and forth
ricocheting off the low-slung clouds
and probing like an instrument in flesh
for the fragments of a former existence.

Off toward a brightening corner of the eye
where insulation draped the power poles
like washing hung out on a line
and the bounding strobes of rescue vehicles
throbbed against a blistered consciousness
the leaden shouts rolled out to him
on a thick wet ball of mist
and slapped against his ear

with a sodden wave of deafness
so that a long lost word like tornado
a word suddenly made flesh
was the only one he let slip past
and leak on down inside
to paralyze the raging in his veins.

When searchers came and stood about
in mud-encrusted boots and pants
ringing him on every side
like lost boys grown cold around a campfire
who gather to discuss their fate
someone brought a sheet of plywood
to slip beneath his shoulder blades
and knelt with those who hoisted him
against his pleas for them to wait
out of the deep mud plaster cast
where he levitated briefly on their hopes
and slid down that last dark tunnel
just as his backbone snapped in two.

Twister: On March 31, 1973, a tornado touched down in Abbeville County, SC, about 9 p.m., traveling northeast from Seneca St. near Calhoun Falls toward the town of Abbeville. It left a path of destruction 200 yards wide and 20 miles long, leaving 6 dead, 12 hospitalized and 450 people homeless. It destroyed 50 homes and damaged an additional 130. A motel owned by J.W. Slaton was demolished on the outskirts of Calhoun Falls near Mud Creek, scattering debris and bodies across the road and into a field for 200 yards. Four victims who were in the motel died. One died in the manner described in the poem. See: *The Press And Banner,* Abbeville, SC, 4-4-1973.

Deer Sign

The dirt sculpture of a doe's track
large enough to put your fingers in
scarred the clear spot in the road
its thick crescents mired to the dew-claws
like a child's print
violating the worked finish of wet cement.

Standing there above its tug and pull
temples pounding with excitement
and eyes frantic to find the blood trail
that completes the vision
of an inaugural adolescent shot
I tried to grasp the truth
waiting just beyond my years
so patient and so camouflaged
mocking me in its silence.

A small pathetic circle
through pine laps and honeysuckle
in an ever-tightening ritual
closed upon this sacred sign
smaller now
perhaps not even fresh
the sun at another angle in its crevices
like a shatterer of worlds
sparing neither the shock nor the cruelty
of a clean miss.

Mr. Fish

He was the same T.J. they said had died
of wounds at Chancellorsville in '63
but he made it home to follow a mule
over root clumps and straggled furrows
in old briar-rimmed sprouting fields
and to age like the leather on his plow-lines
and finally to wear the years right off the rockers
of that front porch chair of his
so that when his wife and only daughter
died of wracking bed-drenched typhus
and were laid out until someone sensible
pressed and pled for burial
he lacked the grace to let them go
but squandered time and family savings
on a crypt of monumental size
so their bodies could lie above the ground
and out of earth's hungering dark.

After rocking through a few more seasons
like some hollow doll-rag effigy
breaking off from it long enough to make
those laden wagon trips out to the spot
to scratch and tamp and rearrange
he walked there with a pry-bar
in the dead of that final night
with all he needed lying there in place
and ripped the hinges from the door
and entered the darkened vault
dragging the rocking chair in with him
before bricking up the opening from inside
by the light of a beeswax candle
and then settling back to wait.

No one goes there now
but for years children stood alone
on the outside of those mortared joints
while their friends waited elsewhere
stood alone there on a dare
and knocked on the bricked-up door
and said, "Mr. Fish, Mr. Fish,
what are you doing in there?"
and he would say, "Nothing at all."

Mr. Fish: Thomas Jefferson Fish is buried in the Memory Hill Cemetery in Milledgeville, GA. There are various versions of his death, though nothing to substantiate the details of it. Mr. Louis Andrews, cemetery historian, entered the vault upon the occasion of its third vandalism many years ago and found the remains of the rocking chair in the crypt. The story of Fish's death, while a Milledgeville legend, is thought also to have been a factual account.

Blackberry Winter

Spring sits on this bleak land
like a new ruler
green-robed and magnificent
impatient to exercise his will
and lift his various scepters
of budding red maple
or blossoming white pear
before the beaten wind-whipped multitude
of later lesser subjects.

Oblivious to the seasonal threats
of perilous flood or withering drought
and eager to reign over us
he wagers extravagantly all his resources
against these treacheries
and heeds not the old warriors
whose fallen cones and needles
lay witness to countless brief
albeit previous rules.

His kind does not survive for long
and is remembered only in the flourishing.
Under the blue sapphire
of a changing and relentless sky
his days will pass
and he will be borne away in rags
with scepters stripped or broken
to some potter's field.

While nature waits and mourns
there will arise from the empire's ruins
of tags and petal-strewn residue
an heir to blasts and frosts
who will build his kingdom from the terraces
and ragged lowly banks
bowed like a servant
going about the farms and fields
in a stained green robe
and he will lead us gently
toward the waning seasons.

The Price of Land

Fe Baker was a slick one
and the day old Lou walked up beaming
and made the last payment on her place
he smiled that possum smile and said
that she had almost paid out
and before she thought she told him
that her debt was paid in full
to which he looked surprised and said
through that surly grin how she
had just called a white man a liar
and went on to tell her
that out of the goodness of his heart
he would forget all about it
and she could pay for the place again.

Remembering her slavery days
and knowing how the likes of Fe Baker
could hold their shadows over her
and steal her hill-top patch of ground
with no more than a word
about her not knowing her place
and being curt and uppity to him
she silently cursed his lying tongue
and went home in a tremble
and stood there by the two oak trees
that marked its shaded entrance
gazing off at the distance
until family came and led her in
away from the rantings of the wippoorwills.

They woke to metal ringing in the morning
and found her with an axe
biting into those big oaks
arms flailing out in massive strokes
and wet white chips pelting the ground
cart-wheeling in all directions.
She fought as hands reached out to her
telling them all to get back
and let her chop the cotton

but they finally got the axe away
before having to put Lou away
in the asylum in Columbia
and stayed on there to pay things out
and sanctify the price of land.

The Price of Land: A.T. McCombs, grandson of Lou Banks, resides on the place that was paid for twice. The 60 acre piece of property is on Hwy. 823 from Abbeville, SC, to Mt. Carmel, SC, near the Mt. Carmel city limits on that road. Lou Banks died in the insane asylum in Columbia, SC, and her family remained to pay the land out of debt. Fe Baker, storekeeper and land owner, is also a subject of interest in the poem, *Hominy Pot.*

The Resistance

Autumn is burning the woods
in partisan fashion
igniting separate fires
that catch on the veils
of early morning
and spread in all directions
like sparks in the wind
wreaking incalculable havoc
and torching everything.

Slipping through the trees
in a trailing robe of leaves
slightly ahead of the bursting patterns
no weed or shrub or lesser form
is spared the brilliance
of its subversive work
which does not fail to let
the summer's dried brown caissons pass
untouched or uncontended.

The Taliaferro Homeplace

The first hand to touch the brick
laid it lovingly in the top course
of a cellar soon to bear
green and groaning timbers
oozing out their substance
to feed a dream-starved hunger
on a hard-scrabble farm;
laid in between the uprooting of stumps
one by one with rope and ox
dirt in the callouses on his hands
proud Virginia in his veins
and a Georgia bounty grant in his trunk.

Fired from his own clay pit
with proper measure of straw and river sand
he had pressed each stubborn lump
into uniformity and order
and had run the straight red courses
alternating headers and stretchers
in an English cross-bond;
fired from an old remembrance
he had added the tuck-pointing groove
to the center of the joints
with the ghostly hand of his father
before washing his mortar-board
in the stream of time.

The next hand to touch it
two centuries after
pried it from the honeysuckle vines
in a sunken place as dank
and odorous as death
risking imaginary bites and scratches
in one desperate unprotected moment
to resurrect it to a lesser purpose.

Turning its pale orange edges to the light
he had no eye for the subtleties
of the craft
and no love for the land —
the tears of the sower
and the shouts of the reaper
and the ring of the mason's trowel
all unbeknownst to him.

Sitting beside the old logging road
where the saplings had been bruised
by the skidder
and stumps shone like gravestones
of an old family cemetery
back in the woods
he poured oil in his chainsaw
and leaned his back against a tree
secure in the abundance of simple possessions
sardines and crackers and a cool thermos
arrayed to his liking
and a brick to scotch the back tire
of his pulpwood truck.

The Taliaferro Homeplace: (pronounced *Toliver*). The homeplace of Benjamin
Taliaferro (1750 - 1821) is located in north Wilkes County, GA, on property now
owned by Champion Paper Company. The remains of a basement and a cemetery
can still be identified. The property is near the Broad River, about three miles north
of Pope's Chapel United Methodist Church, now closed. George R. Gilmer, in his
book, *First Settlers of Upper Georgia,* 1855, describes the house in detail on p. 125.

Statement

Goldenrod flares
pagoda-like
lording over the frost-burned fields
while the blood of autumn
is ankle-deep along the roadside
dripping from the veins of sumac
and splattering the shallow ditches
with its dying glory.

Pollen floats
dream-like
from the golden tops
dusting every lane of air
through which the aging light
of the sun must pass
and lingering
as a reminder that
something will always bloom.

At Delhi

John Lovinggood's old store
is still there in the crossroads
empty now and weathered by the rains
of a hundred springs and the frosts
of as many hard-bitten winters
yawning toward the road
like an old storyteller
who has stayed up too late
but who still has much to tell you.

Crows perch on its ridgerow
and squirrels have wintered in its rafters
but they are as cautious as the mice
living under its broken floorboards
of the old yellow cat
scarred like a war veteran
and blind in one eye
and the last of a long line
which had the run of the place

The first one had just cleaned up the scraps
young Lovinggood had fed it
and had begun to wash its paws
by the door that day
when Dillard Herndon stomped inside
and tried to kick it hard
as he was prone to do
but it dodged behind a feed sack
with a memory of that hated shoe.

He cursed and struck at it again
as it ran across the counter top
just before the gun went off
that shot hot scalding disbelief

straight through the storekeeper's vitals
and bounded out the open door
and into the surrounding cotton fields
where people tried for many weeks
to call it, catch it, kill it
until they made it wild
and said it died in the woods someplace
but it never left.

The story goes that Herndon
blamed the killing on the cat
and told how it had jumped
from the counter to the floor
as cats are prone to do
and struck the gun which fell
and fired the fatal shot
but he was hanged when it was found
that both barrels had discharged
a feat no one believed about a cat
but Herndon who swore to it
just before he swung.

At Delhi: Dillard Herndon (d. 8-17-1900) was the last man hanged in Wilkes
County, GA. Tried and convicted and sentenced for the murder of John J.
Lovinggood (1872 - 1899), Herndon swore to the last that he was innocent. Going
into the store with his shotgun, he asked to purchase a box of shells. When he paid
for them with a $20.00 bill, Lovinggood had to open his safe to make change.
Herndon claimed that he had propped his shotgun against a wall and the cat in the
store caused an accident which led to Lovinggood's death, yet money and other
items from Lovinggood's safe and cash register were found in his possession.
Lovinggood is buried at Pope's Chapel United Methodist Church cemetery in
Wilkes County. His store still stands in the Delhi Crossroads. Herndon is buried
in the nearby Beulah Baptist Church cemetery in Lincoln County.

Catchers

Catchers do their best work at night
stepping into soft feathered whiteness
like old cotton pickers
in a field before moonrise
when the harvest is more felt than seen
and the work more peaceable
so that the catcher can ask the grower
between houses
"You got any more of that good white?"

At once they taste the clinging air
and choke but do not drown
their shallow breaths coming out
close-mouthed and nostril filtered
resisting imaginary dregs
until the stench is gone
and familiar sweetness burns the nose
and tongue
and coats the body with a sensuousness
that brings inspiration to the task.

Reaching under trembling warmth
to gather thirteen birds a throw
they sling them into the open holes
of the tilted cages
with a sleepwalker's practiced grace
waking only when a miss or a drop
kinks up the rhythm
or the forklift jabs in too close
like a red-eyed Lucifer
and kills their night vision.

In deft dream-like sweeps
they churn through the houses
on tireless wind-mill arms
snatching up and spiriting away
all that breathes and lives
emptying out in one night
an entire creation
and then standing idle
in a great loneliness
like dirty-shoed deities
savoring only the ammonia and dust
stirred from their dying world.

Catchers: *meaning chicken catchers.

Respite

Opening the door of the old shed
and entering a fabled time
I sit among the residue
of generations
as fingers of sunlight
reach through the cracks
to fondle old worn-out discs
and harrows.

I breathe the smell of death
of ancient collars
cracked by a half century of sweat
of long-forgotten hay and sweet potatoes
layered in the strata
of shucks and dust.

I feel the touch of it
on the cold white grindstone
broken in its cradle
and the useless stubs of hooks
rusting on the rafters
and I sense its presence
in the memories of killing frosts
and boiling pots
and countless ancient rituals.

Who keeps covenant
with these discarded implements
and brittle pieces of harness?
Who bears the guilt
of sprouts prising out the nails
of the wall boards?
Who sits in reverence
where giants have labored and lost
contemplating their silent toil?

There is no heart for it
among its current tenants
at home in the crevices
where endless scampering
desecrates these shrines
and defiles their altars
where anvils are still bolted.

And I who trespass here
in this dark cramped square
of sacred time and space
must return across its grassy threshold
to a people who have no accumulations
and no memory
and who worship leisure
as their only god.

Mule Talk

When Haywood Pittman took to the sickbed
and his row crops went to grass
his brother Von and all the neighbors
brought their teams to work the fields
and Bartow Barron came with his mule
and stood there by the others
as the work was parcelled out
waiting down to the last
so that no one overheard it
when he leaned close and said to Von Pittman
that he did not work well with other people
and was there a place to go
where he could plow off to himself
in the twists and furrows of his own thoughts.

In a choked-out cane patch on the bottoms
too far gone to save
he found a privacy that suited
and waded into wet sobbing weeds
waist-high in the rank grasses
bent on saving pale spindly stalks
souring from a lack of sun
and hollering at his balking mule
like someone crazed with rage
or loneliness
audible from the higher elevations
where they listened as they worked
through the burden of the day
to shouts and cries ringing from him
made answerable in the language of the mule
who spoke back in unearthly peals
and gained encouragement each time
his owner's voice was heard
by those plodding in their silence
who tried to fathom how one they knew
preferred such conversations to their own.

For The Dry Seasons

When the thirst is so intense
that the air has a parched taste
and the drought is so prolonged
and pronounced with yearning and delirium
that one is driven further
into the barren wastes of want and need
be attentive to the mirth and joy
of the little stream within you
which can quench all doubt
and quell the urges of the flesh
and replenish the shriveled tissues
of the heart.

It is a sufficient well-spring
to gush out upon desperate aching hopes
and emaciated desires
and soak their husks
until they swell again.
Let it be a bursting fountain
which spews its silver contents
into the emptiness of a desert.
Linger there
and find some small refreshment
in the rushing of its waters.

A Home For Heroes

I was there the day Paul Anderson
bent a steel Coca Cola stopper
between his thumb and forefinger
in front of Jake Cooley's filling station
and I watched him awe the crowd
rotund and ominous in black tights
and high-topped leather shoes
when he picked up so much weight
in the high school gymnasium
it cracked the floorboards of the stage
and everyone sighed and marveled
that the strongest man in the world would come
to our school.

And I was there when Lash LaRue
fresh from the dime store comics
played the Anderson County fair
and stood idle between half hour shows
waiting obediently like a dog
for the green plaid barker's signal
that placed him on the toe mark
from which he flicked his whip
and popped those green and white balloons
fastened to a plywood board
and then signed autographs
for wide-eyed boys who did not question
why he ever left the cactus and sage
to come out here.

There was no special lifetime place
where heroes past their prime were kept
encapsulated by protective seals
that would not let them fade or age

91

but in our hearts they gathered strength
and fought and bled
long past the flagging years
they worked the circuses and fairs
and toured the schools
staring down each minor degradation
like a yellow-eyed wolf
cuffed and caged and left in isolation
to languish in its spirit
but never to cower.

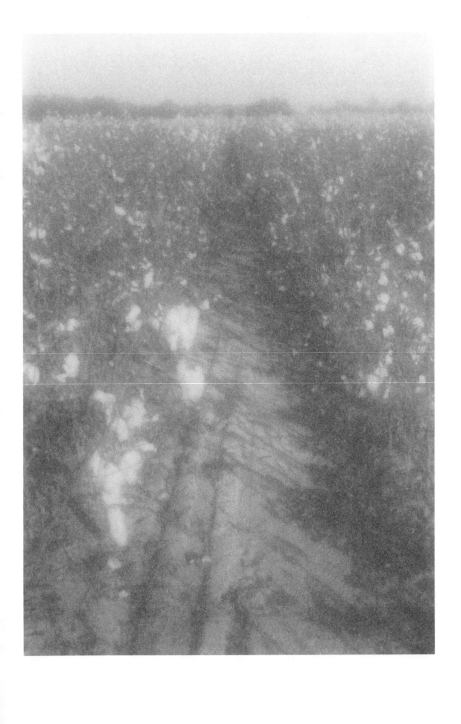

Southland

There are places here
where buildings rub against the notches
of Orion's belt at night
and bathe their bottom portions
in the lights of eight-laned thoroughfares
which stretch beyond their gleaming steel
and on past towns and truck stops
to dim-lit regions
where fox and deer still play.

And there are others
tightly held in fence-dressed acreage
where the air smells of fresh-turned earth
or the soft melt of hayfields
and where old briar-choked ravines
and kudzu patches and power lines
are decorated with rusting farm machinery
that always shines like new
in the moonbeams.

There are hidden places
under the darkened canopies of pine plantations
which once opened to the stars
before the paper companies came
and before clear-cuts and control burns
sucked out wet-weather branches
where the fox-squirrels denned
and drank up the swamps of the wood duck
and the cane cutter rabbit
in brown-needled silence.

Sometimes in the dead of night
on the note of an owl or bobcat screech
a cry goes up from these lands
that is lost in the roar of trucks
and slow cruising cars with loud radios
but it grieves the desecration
of these territories
by the shapers who come and go.

And sometimes when the sky is filled
with winking stars
and the night is loud with crickets
and old sow raccoons walk the creek
in search of mussels
the land can once more be itself
and changes can go unremembered for a time
while we who are the shapers
dissolve ourselves in sleep
and are known for what we are.

We are the dust of dreams
passing through the wind-blown night
gracing unmentionable places
with only the whisperings of ourselves.
We have cut and built and planted
we have killed and bred and rearranged
we have piled it up and torn it down
with our fingers and our machines
and what we have done will come
to nothing.

Out of the gullies and the windrows
and out of the old county landfills
from the poisoned grass on littered roadsides
and the stinking city holding ponds
to the trailer parks and junkyards
forms will fashion and arise
amid blind staggering birds
and soft defective turtle eggs
and the flaking scabs of dying fish
that line the banks of toxic streams.

Beneath the resined roots of the loblolly
below the tine marks of the harrow
under the acres of concrete
and the endless miles of asphalt roads
where earth has been prepared and packed
to purge their memory from the soil
the little hardwood seedlings wait
like bones in the earth
ready to assemble themselves
at the awakening call.

On some fog-drenched acid evening they will come
cracking the hardened surface casings
to propagate across these landscapes
and their harvest will again be borne
in the jaws of the squirrel
and in the beak of the jay
to every distant edge and corner
like seeds in the wind
until it plants and reconstructs
a new and rising South.

Demise Of A Moth

I watched it spin in the headlight beam
a lazy circle as night rushed past
and catch a thread from a fleeting dream
in a crystal trickle down my glass
a tear blurred dry by the wiper blade.

The Homecoming

They had been to Six Flags
and were coming back that night
on the road from Monticello to Milledgeville
tired from the thrill of shocks
and pleasures to the system
and ready to resume an interest
in the mediocre facts about themselves
buried in the footnotes
of an ordinary life
the two girls listening to the drone
of parental undertones in closed communion
blending with the brittle tin
of voices on the local station.

A glimpse of it rushed past
caught in the periphery of the high-beam
and faded on the screens of their retinas
like pink stain on blue litmus
but they all saw it
there on the side of the road
staring into their souls
like a harbinger from another time
with that look in the eyes
of Manassas and Cold Harbor and Seven Pines
and a dull glinting of old steel
from under the dust-covered hat and cape
of a soldier in Confederate gray
a psychic imprint
indelible to the mind's eye
with arms outstretched before them
and pleading on one knee
as if to be remembered to their hearts
and forgiven and released.

As soon as they could find a place
they turned around and headed back

to focus on the piece of ground
so recently beheld in common
and hallowed instantly by what they saw
bodies and brains flooded with sickening fear
but instincts urged and pushed toward a reunion
in the collective unconscious.
No one was there
when they slowed down at the scene
of their approximations
and got out with the motor running
faces flushed hot with blood
to make a hurried search
symbolic in its half-efforts
by a safe proximity to the car
the image dying slowly inside them
as if they had killed it
and sprinkled its fleeting remnants
like ashes in the night.

The ride home yielded further gestures
of wholesale disappointment masking their relief
the tomb-like quiet of the car
punctured by reverenced words in season
and an immediate return visit with the law
who shined his flashlight and found nothing
as stars tilted toward late evening
all part of a delicate conspiracy
and a subtle bid for closure
on the telepathic messages deciphered
declaring how terrible and how touching
and with what split-second display
it had held them frozen in its awe
and how everyone would think them crazy
to believe in such things and to fall
for what was obviously a prank
but failing to disclose how they held it
safe and impotent in their deceit.

The Homecoming. This is a story from the 1970's which occurred on GA State Highway 212 as described. It happened to the C.E. Dunahoo family of Milledgeville, GA. Another story of Mr. Dunahoo's is given in the piece entitled, *The Shining Time.*

First Lessons

While the beagles chase the scent
go over and put your hand
down under the dew-drenched grasses
and feel the warm bed of the rabbit
and wonder how nature contrived
for all of life to feel at home here.

And while the help handles the stiff carcass
left hanging out all night
and trims off the excess fat
go stand by the crackling pot
and taste the ones laid out to dry
and consider how the terror of death
can provide for you.

And while everyone admires the homemade quilt
called The Gentleman's Bowtie
and compliments the wry old woman
go look in her scrap bucket
behind the quilting frame
and marvel at the way the generations
can still teach you with her fingers.

Linthead

After pulling the weekend swing-shift
and slicking back his dirty hair
with water and a comb
he perched there on the porch
of a white clapboard in the village
like those pigeons on the wires above him
cooing and sighing their temporary contentments
and listened to that gospel quartet music
coming from the phonograph just inside the door
breathing in the smell of old bacon grease
which never seemed to leave the house
spidery threads of cotton from the spinning room
still sticking to the starched legs of his overalls
and lint as fine as lunar dust
filling every tiny crater in the skin.

No one knew what was on his mind
or why he picked that night to do it
but after one of those mournful wrenching pieces
by the Happy Goodman Family
he got up and walked back in
to where his wife was folding clothes
and grabbed her bony pipestem wrists
with a grip that could snap a dogwood bobbin
and accused her of stepping out
his wide tear-streaked face a mask of rage
under the naked sixty watt bulb
and a glowering in his eyes
to match the look of the devil.

He left her Maytag-white and crumpled
on the floor by the washing machine
and drove up to the Triangle Cafe
where he got a roll of nickels for the jukebox

and listened to the same song twenty times
then headed out to a deserted spot
on the banks of the Savannah River
and by the light of a clouded moon
in the paroxysms of tormented thought
and with the motor still running
ran a hose from the warm exhaust
through a crack in the back window
and breathed in the thick gray anesthetic
like the aroma of old bacon grease
and took that last deep sleep.

Some fisherman out checking his trot-lines
the next morning found the car
doors locked and glasses up
and blood bubbling from the nose
of its solitary erstwhile occupant
then hurriedly called it in
and a number of them came from work
at the changing of the shift
to view the gaping bloated face
of one they remembered but hardly saw
heavy tremors churning through them as they looked
remembering how he had boasted on lunch breaks
that he could doff and restring faster
than any super on the third
and wondering if they knew
in the incessant blur and din
of spin-bob-weave-shuttle
who any of them really were.

Fire Ants

The old queen hobbles out behind her soldiers
her smouldered mound destroyed
and her ranks thinned down to nothing
from a merciless assault of diesel fuel
flooding the subterranean tunnels of her empire.
In her brief reign she has been sprayed
and gassed and burned and desecrated
only to drag away each time
and lay enough renewing eggs
for the excavations of new and greater castles
and a spurning of memory for the old.
If she survives this latest onslaught
and lives to reap her vengence
and propogate large raging armies
those who tread the bored-up earth
will quicken at her scourge
and curse each stinging step
and the name *solenopsis invicta*
will taste like gall in every throat
when it is spoken in contempt of her.

Lover

The dream was so simple
owning a farm on a county road
somewhere far from town
and keeping it separate
like a mistress
in the anonymity of a second existence
some place to rip and roar out
the joys of self-indulgence.

Some place to renew one's youth and vigor
cleaning out old springs
and making brush piles
on a new ground
some place to give in to temptation
and grow without worry
a covert stand of cotton
whose cash value would never matter
some place with red gullies on the back side
to dump all the broken expectations
accumulating like the unpaid bills
in the family grocery business.

The problem was
it became a reality too fast
and a price was paid
for a sizable piece on the river
with mules and tenants
and too many fence gaps
and all the other complications
required to lead a double life
and make some showing.

There were the occasional nights at home
when the resentment of prolonged absences
building like a newspaper fire
in a woodstove
was registered by the lack of conversation
in the darkness of the porch
amid the churring of crickets
and felt later in the quiet of the bed.

It was the talk for weeks
at the filling station
talk that got back to him
of swapping life under the ceiling fan
for worn-out ground
on which others had taken previous turns
and gained in the bargain
along with vacant time-lined faces
and the soured smell of their shirts
the humiliation of pitiful crops.

"Only a fool," they said,
"would take the land others had used
and pay to be used by it."
They would come by the store
and prop against the dairy case
with those sly knowing grins
like the rusting child
on the Merita bread sign
in the bottom of the door screen.

That and the resistance felt
in the stubborn hard-packed fields
so in character
with the reputation of the place
finally caused him to get rid of it
and go back to the chair
with the sagging wicker bottom
robbed of one last ridiculous aspiration.

On late afternoons
when sweat stains the band
on the Panama covering the bald spot
and the bulge around his middle
reminds him of the rings in old trees
and kids deliberating over penny candy
pester him as much as the gnats
on the over-ripe bananas
he'll still dream about that place
and think to himself how life's
a bitch
but a pretty bitch.

The Joy Of Lesser States

It is good to be as sparrows
pecking in the roadside gravel
or a peeper in the rushes
near a drainage culvert
noticed but unremembered
and more convincing in our lowliness
day by day

or as a tenant farmer's child
pulling fodder from the stalks
in stubborn clinging fields
accepting roles beneath us
and finding in this barren life
a narrow rug on which to lie
and dream the dreams of selflessness.

The Shining Time

The years that dim the names and faces
have lost sight of his
and no one wants to find the grave
and read the stone
but there was a time
when his grandson was hip-high
that he took those little hands in his
and felt the web of sprouting seed-warts
and sent him inside to fetch
the black frock coat on the peg
with the long silver needle
gleaming in the lapel.

There in the clean-swept yard
under the chinaberry
as a dust devil stirred on the road
and there was no other noise
he pulled it from the cloth
and held it so it sparkled
like a new-found truth
in the righteousness of words
that said it had the power
to heal all that it touched
if one believed it in the heart
and did not doubt its gift.

When he got the nod
and saw the look of wide-eyed wonder
glisten on that trusting face
he spoke in soft flat tones
and touched the needle to each wart
so that the will to cast them out
passed through its shaft and left
a residue of promise on each one

and a pledge from him to wear the coat
until all of them were gone
and the tiny hands were free
of their hated blemishes.

In two weeks they had faded
back into pink pliant flesh
just like the memories of him
that have slipped themselves free
of their mortal bonds
and vanished like ghosts
with this one among the last to go.
Some said he could talk out fire
and staunch the flow of blood
and conjure out the poison of a bite
but the one who trusted recollects
how this was his shining time.

On The Grounds Of Central State

There are gentle slopes here
graced by lawns and shrubs and campused trees
falling away like green fronds
from the Powell Building
and shimmering
under the serenity of its white-washed dome.

God bless these decorated slopes
but let it be written somewhere
that once there lurked behind these peaceful walls
terror in its starkest form
and shrieks enough to blunt the razor edge
of every midnight
and sweaty grips enough to rust and bend
these white-washed window bars.

And let a prayer be said
for all the souls once warehoused here
who never felt a mother's touch
or a friend's hand of kindness
and who never knew the miracle of thorazine.

Let someone mention where they have gone
the ones not claimed by relatives
who lie in nameless graves
with metal stobs that are all alike
on a distant corner of the grounds
that no one manicures
sunken down to a final loneliness
where they do not scream or cry.

And let a word go forth
to their contemporary counterparts
distributed in the surrounding compounds

and locked in their various drugs and therapies
which will speak assurances
to the unabated howls of anguish
that beat the walls of consciousness
but are so muffled and suppressed
that no one guesses or suspects
the reaches of their darkness
or their power.

And let it speak as religion to them
in the soft-lit rooms
and in the tiled and disinfected places
where they cannot see the neat boxed hedges
and the falling slopes
or any angle of that tranquil white-domed Mecca
for the insane.

And let it tell them this

Fear not that you are small
or that giants will overtake you
or that you will stand alone.
Stride out before their shadows
with feeble sling to aid you
and stoop down by the icy brook
and grasp the shining stone.

On The Grounds Of Central State: The Powell Building was one of the first
facilities built at Central State Hospital, Milledgeville, GA, which, during its
history, housed more than 12,000 patients and employees in peak years. The
hospital, located two miles south of the town of Milledgeville, opened in 1842 and
was the state's first psychiatric hospital and still administers care to approximately
2000 patients.

The Dawn Patrol

They boldly go while morning stars are out
in tight formation three abreast
through the no man's land of empty streets
in a hazy subdivision grid
mined with lamp post bats and barking dogs
and the smells of curb-side garbage bins
risking life and limb to celebrate
this sacred sisterhood of slender waists
that has become the morning constitutional
designed to punish sagging cellulite
and shrink to nothing tree-trunk thighs
while resurrecting back from faded days
the lasting side-effects of maidenhood.

Bedecked with sunscreen on their cheeks
head-set turned on, squeeze-jug in tow
they rag the scale to an oldies tune
adjusting sweat-bands, changing stride
each time they make their pass
by early coughing cars and back-up lights
and the mystique of darkened doorways
that call to mind "somewhere in France"
flipping their jumbo tennis skirts
and counting cadence with the gum they pop.
See them glisten, watch them glow
leaving to widen in their wake
a vapor trail of Giorgio.

Double-Take

The people waiting for the train
with rice to throw and roses
standing on the platform like a cast
ready for its dress rehearsal
made their final coat and tie adjustments
there at the Oconee station
when the east-bound out of Macon
called the Shoo-fly
rounded the turn and slowed on its air-brakes
its gray plume dropping like a shroud
ahead of it on the grinning bystanders
deafened by the grate of agonizing steel.

Stepping down from a passenger coach
sun-browned hands coiling a grip around the brass
Bartow Barron braced the crowd alone
and watched the faces fall on those
who had spent the balance of the afternoon
to be on hand to greet his bride
or more distinctly put
to be among the first to see
exactly who would wed a man
whose voice would shift from high to low
in every verbal interchange
and whose conversations were more freely heard
and valued by the yard stock
than by the likes of humankind
his being more in league and tenor
with the beasts of the field
and of limited and questionable resource.

Sensing at once the cruelty in their kindness
he thanked them for the welcome
and confided in a high-low tone
how his bride would be delayed two weeks
dangling the prospects of her coming
like enticing bait before them
words drowning in the departing steam
and knowing they would have to go back home again
where they would be compelled to think again
and wash and dress and pick the flowers again
before coming back to wait again
and get their satisfaction
while he got his.

The Breakfast Club

Mosquitoes singing over the pond scum
draw their careless circles
on the crystalline panels of a summer's day
where neither time nor purpose
exchanges fraternal greetings
with the cloud and swarm of delegations
milling in attendance.

Homing in on the minuets and trajectories
of infinitesimal creatures
tracing their arcs on the windows
of a diamond sky
a frog presides over the ceremonies
like a stuffy parliamentarian
squatting upon a podium of moss and slime
eye-slits turned upward in the sun
and coiled tongue poised to catch
those it rules out of order.

There are others drawn to these proceedings
in the high-polish glisten and shine
studded with biplane drones of the snake-doctor
or gnats hissing from their blackened funnel
as turtles from the churned-up bottom
and redwings riding down the cattails
converge upon a sudden gleam of light
and, in the turning of a wing-beat or a moment,
become the first to broach
the serving line.

Hominy Pot

Whippoorwills were out that night
old man Fe Baker's store was robbed
singing their death threats in unison
condemning those miserable souls
stumbling like drunks over sacks and boxes
while poverty's other children slept.
Arms burdened and stinging with salt pork
pockets strangling on candy and chewing tobacco
they rose like pilfering crows
when a floor-board creaked
and left the place a shambles.
One braver than the rest came back
and burned out the ledger pages
of his white creditor
leaving a smoking candle
to touch off its mischief in the cracks
of the leather binding
so that daylight broke on the old bald head
of Fe Baker weeping by the ruins
gazing down into them like he would
a smouldering hickory pit
and the whippoorwills stopped.

Tut Danford knew who did it
and they were out again that evening
like choristers appointed to the graveyard quiet
shrilling their emphasis from the woods
as he stood between two crowds
receiving more attention than a dead man
and swelling up with it
when the constable used Mister with his name.
The black folks whispered,
"Hush, Tut! Hush!"
while the white ones said,

"Talk on, Danford! Talk on!"
And he talked on in a natural pride
talking so fast he talked up the dust
in the middle of the road.
He talked on until someone broke and ran
and he talked on after an arrest was made.
As the darkness and the whippoorwills
and his tongue got thicker
Tut talked on
and talked himself right into
the hominy pot.

It was waiting for him
that next night as he walked along
looking up at the sky's deep velvet
and humming a tune.
The stars came out
just as the others did who grabbed him
and dragged him to the river
where he grasped a tree so tightly
the bark came off in his hands
as he was pulled begging and pleading
to the mouldered ground.
They tied his hands and feet
and gagged that talking mouth of his
and, sliding down the steep Savannah bank,
held him in the flatboat
while the rock was fastened to his chest
and then like ghosts in dreams
they poled out to that suck-hole
at the mouth of Russell Creek
and dropped him in.

It took a week to lay the talk to rest.
Some said he had run off
while others guessed the hominy pot
but all agreed that if a body knew
it would not tell
although such a body did.
On a day when the whippoorwills were shrieking
chiding those who had almost forgotten
up from the whirlpool's gullet

where the Confederate seal was tossed
on that mad ride out of Abbeville
and from which no man's bones returned
Tut shot straight and true
swelled a little larger than in life
with that Igratic gas inside
and bringing the rock up with him.
It was sundown when he crested out
five days later than Jesus
but since those who did it had not talked
and no one had the straight of things
he thought he would come back
one more time
and tell it for himself.

Hominy Pot: This story was told by an aged black descendant of Tut Danford who was bound and thrown into this whirlpool at the mouth of Russell Creek, McCormick County, SC, by confederates of the blacks who robbed and burned Baker's Store in the town of Mt. Carmel. It is said that the rock taken from the chest of the body of Danford was kept for many years in the Abbeville County Courthouse. The Hominy Pot is thought to have been the watery burial spot of the Confederate Seal, tossed by the fleeing cabinet of Jefferson Davis when they evaucated Abbeville.

Heart-Shorn

My hopes sometimes remind me
of gray kudzu vines
spread out across faded winter earth
like the hair of an aged widow
on her death-bed.
They have enlarged in recent seasons
only to be bitten back
in the relentless saga
of harsh competing winds
and the silence
of appointed but indiscriminate frosts.
They have become a brittle labyrinth
of desires
embracing vain affections
turned as cold as spewed-up earth.

My hopes were once like pliant tentacles
which covered the red worn-out soil
striving to possess everything
and knowing no boundaries of containment
as they grew and fed upon their dreams.
They extended their tender feelers
in all innocence and compulsion
creeping at first
then overrunning and burying the fence posts
and strangling out the vetch and foxglove
without knowing that their famished root
could never support their joy.

Blue Winter

Leaves missing
from the green tree
that shaded half the yard
the skeletons of kites
caught in the boughs
resembling crucifixes
the trunk scarred
with old wood carvings
and smooth scar-tissued bark
where the names have healed
frozen limbs on electric wires
like numb fingers on old strings
these things can be tolerated
but a stump
leaves nothing to the imagination.

Wind blew over the well's base
where the yard began
like lips on an empty bottle
and frozen water
in the bucket bottom
was the proper mounting
for a black leaf
spread out like a butterfly
under glass
ice wedged the holes
of the brick that built the flower bed
and stems rattled
like dry bones
and the yard stretched
until snow fell as dingy
as thick cotton lint
covering the tracks
of those who came and went
swinging their lunch boxes

in cuffed overalls
and even then
the yard never stopped.

Under an old washtub
where grass was white and stiff
lay scattered green pieces
of a plastic toy
crushed one spring
by a bicycle wheel
and the yard ended
at age fifteen
when long legs found the edge
which met the road
and imagination ended
on the cracked face
of a child's discarded doll
left in a ditch
with no hair
and one eye missing.

The smokestack world
beyond the house
and up a graveled hill
led to rows of painted windows
tinted blue at night
and sleeveless men in silhouette
behind their massive panes
and the hum
of warm well-oiled machines
like a siren song
sung through the bricks
and down the village back-alleys
taunting old men
huddled by stoves
with their backs hunched
from standing thirty years
at looms and spinning frames
and tempting the young
in bed and cradle
with narrow visions
of what to be.

The house sat vacant
a ragged nest
abandoned by its young
door-screen sagging
power cut from the lines
and plywood in its windows
a husk with its family gone —
died — moved out —
stolen away in the night
to beat the debt
at the company store
as quick and transitory
as their dreams
which never rose
above the barren truth
that everything must change
yards must shrink
people have to die
children come of age
but the mill
goes on forever.

Visits With The Dead

1

We must give up our winter ways
we who have watched our faces change
in dim and yellow window panes
faint with the light of other days
who braced front steps rosy-cheeked and young
in winter clothes on long-sleeved winter nights
and passed blocks of brittle houses icicle-strung
pounding walks with muffled feet
and running up and down dead dark streets
under a necklace made by lamp post lights
running below glazed rooftops of the town
feeling our fingers numb and blush
from pulling icicles down
past the flurry of our own heart beats
then waiting for an avalanche of sound
to catch us in its sickening rush
we who slipped and slid with stockings on our heads
in hopes that something might be kept
and tumbled weak and jaded to our beds
while snow brushed out our footprints as we slept.

2

The evening freeze has settled on old snows
and where the mill houses stand in their dirty rows
a gray dust mingles with the white
on this last cold crust of winter nights
a third shifter slides and scrapes the street
ice crystals stab his feet and bruise
the worn-out bottoms of his summer shoes
the evening wraps him in its brown bedsheet
he shudders on to work stooped-down and old
crunching with his lunch box up the hill
warmed by the electric humming of the mill
and the steam coming out of the air-wash flume
beneath the yellow-lighted spinning room
cutting away the last thick slab of cold
a thaw will leave spring odors
of pigeons buried where the supers park
in melting streets the strain of motors
picking the frozen lock of dark
will break the silence of the snow
and make slush of the silver puddles
and we will laugh as the workers huddle
some spring morning for reasons they do not know.

3

The day we burned the Christmas tree
old mistletoe and popcorn strings
and a broken manger were among the dead
numbered among ineffectual things
no longer silver-strung or wired in red
the semblance that we dreaded most
shivered like a green and dying ghost
stripped of tinsel, ball and bell
it scattered glitter in the dead December
surviving each of the precious days
down to the simple cedar smell.

Of this disposition I remember
while our old newspapers blazed
the journey made in winter weather
pulling it out the door together
and dragging it over the yard's white shell
a frozen execution smile
was on our faces as we marched
while the plastic manger curled and parched
by paper gravestones in the rubbish pile
and let it prick us when our bodies quivered
from standing on its springing spine.

By fire we held it while the green fir withered
and listened as the branches cried and cracked
and the black ribs rubbed our fingers raw
we poked the burnt-out skeleton and saw
its charred bones smoking and felt no pain
standing there in the sun's soft light
but we will hold this conversation again
on some midnight.

Tobe Hester

They closed him down in twenty-two
with a petition signed into law
and the cock-fighting on the island ceased
and the gamblers no longer came to town
with their money-filled suitcases
to bet on the pitted games.
The last box-car load of his "Big Reds"
hit the bright rails of the C. & W. C.
for Mexico that same year
emptying out the remaining pens and houses
and leaving a Negro by the name of Snowball
who had named the games and fed them
and fitted the fighters with gaffs
to stand there weeping by the tracks
for an era that had forever gone
the way of snake-oil and traveling shows.

Heeled tight enough with wealth and legendary
he died not too long after that
though his dying took a little time
which he and Snowball spent taking the flat
and poling over to the island
just to stand there by the sand pit
always soaked pink with blood
on those breezy crowd-filled nights
and recollect how he had never pulled
a losing cock out of a fight
letting it go down valiantly
with its head pecked to a pulp
rather than penning it back up
to be seen before the others
no longer proud but spiritless
scratching out its days like a brood hen.

Squatting down in the pit's ring
and currying its bottom with a board
like he always did it in the old days
he thought that he would rather go out
like a bird he trained once
a close hitter past his full sharpness
and slightly razor-cut on the beak
giving the appearance of a crack
to improve the betting odds
a silent fighter flushed and ready
with short-heel gaffs needle sharp
puffed out to meet death head on
in full strut and not utter a sound
a three-time winner doomed to fall
before the spurs of younger gamer birds
but given one last sporting chance.

Tobe Hester: Samuel J. "Tobe" Hester lived on the old Charleston and Western Carolina railroad about four miles south of Calhoun Falls, SC. His famous chicken ranch drew many people to the area. It is said that the Mexican bandit, Pancho Villa, was there in 1911 and bought game chickens from him on that and other occasions. Town pressure against both state governments (South Carolina and Georgia) finally brought an end to the famous chicken fights that took place on an island in the Savannah River, which neither South Carolina or Georgia claimed as their territory. See: "Cockfighting Sport Steeped in Tradition," by Lester W. Ferguson, *The Press And Banner And Abbeville Medium,* 5-1-1991, p. 4.

The Spider Man

Thumbs hooked in the chain-link
and eyes peering out
half-closed
almost lizard-like
he does not think of freedom now
but of the little rain spiders
whose dew-filled webs
dot rank humid clumps of grass
on the high red bank
bare inches from the galvanized wire.

In the din behind him
other prisoners exert themselves
at volleyball
in orange vests the county provides
the tap-tap of the ball's rhythm
embedded in his consciousness
like the countless cigarette butts
to be shuffled through each day
in the yard.

Taking his cue from a big one
walking on the symmetrical underside
like the lowest form of Adam
inspecting a new garden
he disassociates himself
from shaven heads and ringworm sores
and all surrounding disgust
and grips the metal mesh
with toes and fingers
and leaves the ground.

He does not think of freedom
as he tries a familiar boundary
with a new-found transcendence
and pantomimes on a larger scale
the creature who is Lord and Master
of a select stretch of universe
reserved for itself, alone.

Clinging there
like a rare specimen on a grid
number thirty-eight
whose papers say, slightly retarded,
achieves the perfect vision
as the cold nub of a stick
freezes the back of his neck
and words beckon from a lost world —
"Boy, come on down here now
before you hurt yourself."

A Sprig of Acacia

When they gave Wink Maxwell a Masonic funeral
the Baptist preacher had a burden for it
and out of his own Biblical ignorance
refused to do the reading at the grave
leaving it to the chaplain of the Lodge
and Irv Pruitt who was Worshipful Master
to give their brother a good going off
Irv reading pages from the Brock's Manual
enlarged on the photocopier so he could see
the words without his reading glasses.

When he got to that part about the sprig
which Masons usually wear on the lapel
and then deposit in the open grave
but which Leon the new Junior Warden
summarily forgot to bring with him
this being his first dutiful and solemn occasion
a panic hit the aproned ranks
and bowed heads swiveled instantly
to the only likely substitute closeby
a lightning-struck trunk-split cedar
at the far end of the cemetery
so browned-out from the strike
its green boughs bristled at the top
like the neck hair of the dying.

Irv's brother Heck and Demp Wilson
who was Senior Deacon of the Lodge
walked off in that direction
while Hoyt Elrod got a ladder
from his Tri-County EMC pick-up
and hoisted it at shoulder's length
to keep from scratching the parked cars
before angling off behind the others
and finally propping it on a lower limb.

It would not do for anyone but Heck
to make the pilgrimage through dried nettles
and cut out the last lingering symbols
of the gift of everlasting life
warding off others who volunteered to climb
with declarations of his wanting to be remembered
as the one who did it for Wink.
About halfway up a limb broke off
under the toe of his right dress boot
the sound of it carrying like a rifle shot
and Heck crashed out on his back
snapping dry sticks all the way down
and landing in a solid lump
red-faced and scratched and spooning for air
like a large-mouthed fish.

Considerable time had slipped the knot
and shadows were deepening
before they got Heck in the evac unit
and roared off in the afternoon
at full tilt and siren
leaving Irv Pruitt to finish the ceremony
without the customary toss of evergreen
the widow being restless and impatient
for a reprieve in the excitement
and Wink being the only Son of Light
to be sealed tightly shut
and pointed toward that Celestial City
and its walls of jasper
without a green and hallowed emblem
to brook his immortal passage.
So mote it be!

Spring Offensive

March winds announce
the debut of yellowbell along the roads
and thrift that lines the southern banks
below the dooryards.
Birds call from the privet hedges
that sport their new and unkempt growth
to echoes in the dense brush
where all the indigent grays and browns
are undergoing metamorphosis.
Color has trickled out from the lowliest
of winter forms
like careless splatter
from an artist's brush.

There are different manifestations
in the kingly arches of the tree line
where a deep contrition haunts the boughs.
Only the maple tips, swollen and red-hued,
betray signs of premature expression
and they will be among the first to endure
the cruelties of spring's capricious moods.
The rest stand naked-limbed and vacant
their only tenants a last dried leaf
and cold green leather balls of mistletoe
as they hesitate before a season
which pledges light and warmth.

As sure as guards are dropped
and fields begin to green and luxuriate
and flies begin to hatch
there will come a darkened sky
to spill its brittle fury
on flocks of heavy-breasted robins
skidding to the ground like planes
with over-loaded cargo bays
and lock the world once more in disbelief
from which it shrinks and sighs and waits.

The Drownings At Harper's Ferry
April 4, 1920

At any other time
she would have exercised discretion
enduring larks and laughing innocence
like a maiden aunt
who understands impatient youth
but on that Easter afternoon
she was cold and brown and sullen
swollen out of her banks
and carrying that menstrual odor
that is always on the river
after a rain.

The instant they stepped on the flat
and pushed away with the pole
her ire was stirred
and she knew she would kill them
and she did it, too!
just like she did in the flood of '08
and the earlier one
which took a house and two screaming children
off Goat Island
and hid them in the mud
on her bottom
her with all that passion
and not an ounce of pity.

Warned not to cross her
by one who knew her vexing mood
those older put it aside
and gave in to the others
remembering it again mid-way
when the cable post pulled out
on the Carolina side
and swung the flat downstream

where it shuddered and thrashed
like a hooked shad
until she pulled it down.

Some of them went clinging to it
and quickly drank in her rage
sucking it into their lungs
before the terror could burst their hearts.
Others fought her power
struggling to breathe and shout
and justify in their minds
the impossible act of death
while she amused herself with them.

There was one scene immortalized
by the one who dragged himself
from her icy bosom
in which the married pair
beheld each other for a final time
eyes speaking old eternal words
as the last bows, bonnets and starched collars
were swallowed by her muddy waters
becoming the only good memory to linger
in the days that followed
when friends and family lined the banks.

For about five days
it looked as though she had kept them all
but her blood-lust subsided
and she grew tired of them
and began to give them up
their stiff black hulks
rising from her depths
as far downstream as Millwood
where an idle and curious few
still looked for floaters.
Nine broke the surface
in twice as many days
but she kept young Charlie
from being blown on the bottom currents
by fastening him in the snags
of a cavern under her banks,

and he's there yet!
And, God knows, there have been
so many others.

Oh, my terrible Savannah!
Who but she could grieve
every heart who loved her
and cause the Resurrection Day
to be mourned for a generation
in the town of Lowndesville?
Who could count the times
she has turned so quickly on us all
just to vent her spite?
You see her now when she is old and settled
with her skirts smoothed down
but in her day
she was a fickle lady.

The Drownings At Harper's Ferry: On Easter Sunday, April 4, 1920, nine persons drowned at the ferry crossing on the Savannah River between the towns of Lowndesville and Calhoun Falls, SC. The victims were W. Lester Waters, Lollie S. Waters, Alice Meschine, Charlie Meschine, Inez Manning, Robert I. Manning, Annie L. Manning, Allie Bradshaw and Lucy Bradshaw. All but one are buried at the Presbyterian cemetery in Lowndesville, SC, though the missing child who was never found is listed on the marker. See: *True Stories Of The Savannah,* by H.T. Cannon, a local pamphlet published some years later to record the tragedy. The ferry is now under the waters of Russell Lake.

Night Rider

In the coldness of the driver's seat
the engine not yet warm enough
to thaw the chill
clinging like a hand in death
to vinyl seats and steering wheel
I waited out the first few frosty breaths
until the green light in the panel
winked off
before touching a switch
in star-lit darkness
and bringing life to the blower fan.

When he dropped on a thread of silk
from the right front visor
like a gray and crumpled ball
of carpet fuzz
brittled by the season
the filament he was riding
ended at the heater vent
where warm air billowed it
out and away from the opening.

Poised on the current and illuminated
in the glow of the dashboard
like a performer on the high wire
the ball unraveled
in a snarl and abundance of legs
moving and kicking with joy
and revelry of warmth
and revealed its flexing contents —
an arachnid
dancing in the life of a moment
before climbing back up the string
and awaiting cold oblivion.

Ivy Gates

After you have seen the grave
of the mother of Langdon Cheves
cold and gray and by itself
and visited the church at Cedar Springs
and toured that mud-red wonder
that is called Clark's Hill
and stopped at the metal marker
for the old French settlement
"down aroun' Barh-doh"
and eaten your box lunch on the benches
of the park at Little Mountain
you must travel one more road
and you must go to Ivy Gates.

The old woman in the gown and bonnet
with buckles on her shoes
will meet you at the iron fence
and tell you not to touch anything
as she points out flowers and ferns
in the old wash-pots by the porch
and talks to them like babies
and finally lets you go inside
her mind, her life, her solitary rooms
to see the world that she has kept
dark and polished just for you
to view and smell but not to touch.

She will talk of her people
who never came back from the war
and name the animals that are gone
and show you the high four-poster
canopied in the upstairs bed-room
on which some of her family died
and some were born

then take you back outside
and wind the well bucket for you
and let you sip
her love, her pain, her spirit
from a yellowed drinking gourd
but not too much!
Not too much!

Ivy Gates: Fourth grade field trips from the school in Calhoun Falls, SC, in the 1950's included local historical sites in Abbeville and McCormick counties as well as a trip to the then-new Clark's Hill Dam and Reservoir. Novel sites included the grave of Mary Langdon in Abbeville County, mother of Langdon Cheves, the first Secretary of the U.S. Treasury and head of the U.S. Bank; the French settlement of Bordeaux in McCormick County; the A.R.P. Church at Cedar Springs in Abbeville County; and the house called, Ivy Gates, in the Long Canes section of McCormick County, near Troy, SC. The house was owned at that time by Miss Clara Wideman who taught school in Troy and who allowed children to tour her house and property which was kept as it was in olden times.

Late Hunt

In the slate-gray November
when game is not moving
and a dead limb falling anywhere
desecrates the silence
a hunter tramps through leaves
knee-deep in a darkening hollow
engaged in the illusion
of a private and holy war.

Compelled to stalk deserted trails
with their soft blackened ribbons
spreading out beneath him
he goes cautiously along
intent on tracking down
elusive pieces of himself
which always lie a step ahead.

Heaving with his shoulders
against a paralyzed sky
his aspiration is to gain
the stark and distant ridges
driving out before him
in the stamping of his boots
the fierce beast of loneliness.

There are instances
in the walk toward evening
when a trained eye will catch the truth
like a glint on a gun barrel
and hold its bead long enough
to cause a rending in the flesh.
Love is the highest joy
and the greatest dread of all.
Underneath the hot and gnawing lust
to kill or capture
it is hunted hardest and feared most.

There is never light enough
to find the way completely
or to carry out such hopes and threats
when all grows still.
It is always best
to go back spent and empty
and contemplate from darkness
the bright and terrifying prospects
of tomorrow's luck.

Helton

There is some small reverence now
gliding his car over silk-smooth fields
but it was all hell-bent on a tractor
bleary-eyed and none to help
back there in the nineteen fifties
and long sweltering afternoons
choking in dust from the hay combine
on a three-and-a-half-mile stretch
with its mile-wide frontage at the river
where through emerald waves
he sweated the salt out of the hard years
and two hundred bushels to the acre
on the corn-field bottoms.

Sometime in the pleasure of his heydays
he stood by and watched the pieces
of that simple vision swallowed up
by those who scooped down like false gods
to make the lake and build the power plant
and regulate the flood plain at the dam
drowning his crops like babies every season
and smothering the bottom land with mud
while precious topsoil slipped away
to lie downstream in gagging silt
alongside the glistening promise
that their creations would make him heir
to everlasting benefits.

The final shame did not sink in
before he was compelled to set out pines
to staunch the river's flow
and they tried to buy the right-of-way
to run a power line across his fields
and extend steel tentacles of a monster

already bent on devouring his farm.
On his refusal to comply they sent
their death angel to condemn his land
and run rough-shod over life-long passions
until he stared him right down the barrel
and solemnly swore to blow his head off
if one pole sprouted on his place.

The project was diverted with an elbow
to his bridgeless neighbor's line
where the cable stretching finally stopped
dead against the river's crumbling bank.
When they trespassed to use his bridge across
he had the sheriff come from town
and make one hundred forty-three arrests
and beard the guile of Georgia Power
but dropped the case before the trial
when they agreed to move from sight
all pre-existing poles and run
a buried line to grant him light and heat
and some small reverence now.

Helton: James B. Helton, Jr., still resides on his farm in Baldwin County on GA State Highway 112. He actually resisted Georgia Power Company officials who wished to place power poles on his property and had those who trespassed arrested. The matter was settled out of court as described.

The Lure Of Baited Fields

It is the season
for killing doves.
There will be gatherings
in the fields
of those who wait
among the rich temptations
of seed and grain
for the darkening flocks
to descend and lift
losing some of their number
without protest or deviation
from their repetitive procedure.

My heart waits
like the doves on wires
believing all the promises
displayed before it
like those lavish fields
but knowing
that it participates
in the elaborate deceits
of nature
which lends it
as a voluntary target
for these predatory instincts —
and chooses
in the moment of destruction
to fly willingly.

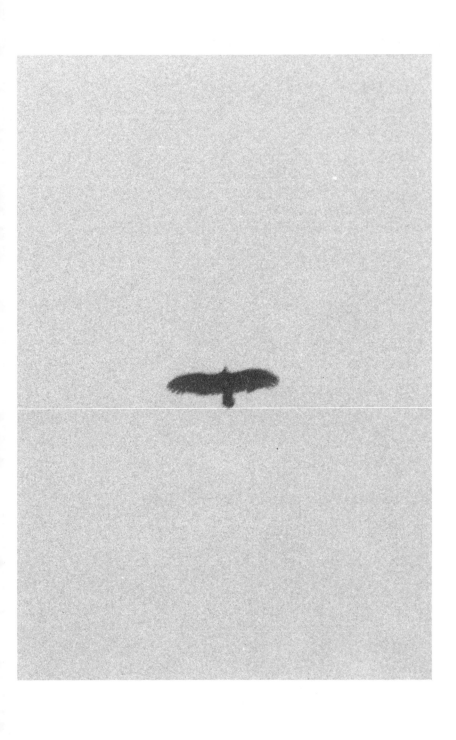

Greene Sheppard's Departure

Jefferson County, Georgia
September 10, 1861

The morning he left for the army
the crow lit on the post
the same way it did every morning
and the buck took the same worn path
to water
looking up as it always did
when he stepped across the threshold
only this time
his foot touched down
on a world that had changed
and everything seemed crisp and new.

His wife and children came behind him
tugging at his memories
as he fought off the feelings
and saw through burning eyes
the knotted well rope
he had meant to fix
knowing it would be better for them all
if he could just walk off
and not have to face them.

But out in the yard
he gathered them and took
one last look into their streaming eyes
and held them fiercely
then headed down the road
past dying morning glory vines
and the cool spot where the road dipped down
and on into history's faded pages.

When he was gone
the children tumbled out the sheds
and took what chicken coops they owned
to put across his tracks
and keep some remnant of him
not knowing that the wind
would eat at them underneath
and the mud would ebb from them
after the fall rains
and scatter them in all directions
and that Virginia's thirsty ground
would drink up everything remaining.

Greene Sheppard's Departure: Sheppard's name appears, along with Elijah and J.F. Shepherd, on the Muster Roll of Company I, 28th Regiment, Georgia Volunteer Infantry, Army of Tennessee, C.S.A. Sheppard enlisted from Jefferson County, GA, and the company was called "Jefferson Greys." The story of his departure from home is told in the book of a descendant, W.J. Hardin, entitled, *Believe It Or Not, It Happened In Georgia,* p. 21.

Applejack

In a shed out back
behind the chicken houses
a world is coming together
as a man named Taterbug
brings things to a boil
and takes himself back
and you with him
to a time when the best was kept
in stone crocks and blue mason jars
the clear liquid calvados
as precious as that Bible nard
your grandmother used to read about.

He was born for this
born to sit for hours
beside the thin stream trickling out
from the bottom of the coil
remembering how it tasted
when the jug first passed
and fire hit the back of his throat
born to recite dreamy images
of those long dead
who laughed and loved him simply
and still cling to him
like the odor in his clothes.

Capping off the best of life at 105 proof
he writes off calculations on the back
of a used-up Blue Horse tablet
and flips the pages back
to his daddy's figures
reminiscing each old batch
before visiting the barrels
to whiff the heady fermentation

where the mother has come and gone
and nudge a dead rat from the walk-space
with the toe of a worn-down hobnail
and the tenderness of a sage among spirits.

He knows there is more to it
than working up unsold apples
or having enough for his own use.
The essence of who he is
has also filtered through the cheese-cloth.
He has never sold it
and would be hard-put to find anybody now
knowledgeable enough to give it to.
He knows it is his way
of being with the old folks
but ask him why he does it and he'll say,
"I'm just making a little Christmas."

A Glimpse Of Finitude

From the deep clean blue
of a winter afternoon
a vulture's shadow taints the ground
from where it hovers
like a black kite on the air currents
invisible and lost in a starburst
of squinting up at the sunlight.

Revolting in its inferences
yet an acceptable part of the landscape
it is a living reminder
of the crepe which hangs
above each final fetid hope
an abiding symbol which intervenes
and bears every succulent joy away
on the rustle of a wing.

Under its lazy spiral
a world turns in review
and beady eyes envision
every eventual outcome
while feathered avarice discloses
a marvelous capacity to wait
before dropping gently down
to pick up on remaining portions
of transitory dreams and sins.

In simple everyday exchanges
of outer and inner nature which transpire
at every coordinate of the earth
scavengers in their relentless sweep
guided by visual and aromatic principles
perform the rite of cleansing
until all remnants
of familiar cherished flesh are gone
and the last circumference left
is where a bone or two lie scattered.

Moonlight Bridge

The night the train derailed
Jimmy Ray and Bonnie Sue parked about midway
idling the motor to keep the heater running
and then switching off and listening
to the noises over on the main highway
before rolling up the glasses
and meeting in the middle of the seat
to rehearse their awkward declarations
with nervous stomachs and sweaty hands.

After she slapped him once
with that taped-up class ring he gave her
and he turned on the light to show her
the red welt it left
and to gain some sympathy
they came together in a strangle-hold
lips locked and eyes closed
and shoes sliding in the wrappers
from the Little Star Cafe
still on the floorboards.

Like two statues melted together
they pressed against each other
retasting burgers, shakes and fries
and fogging up the glasses
with their heavy breathing
until Jimmy Ray had to stop
and blow his nose
which disgusted Bonnie Sue
who said they ought to go
and that her feet were getting cold.

But Jimmy Ray started right back in
renewing his intentions
until Bonnie Sue got mad
and pushed his hand away
and told him to "quit-it!"
He just smiled and went ahead
thinking it was that psycho-thriller
they had watched at the drive-in
that made her touchy
about being there on the bridge.

Neither of them heard it coming
but when a south-bound out of Abbeville
running on a clear signal
topped the notch there under the bridge
the slack ran in about half-way back
and boxcars jumped the tracks
belching out plywood and color televisions
and palet loads of beer
the explosions and after-shocks
vibrating through the bridge
like the end of the world had come.

Unable to see out the steamed-up windows
or to tell why the bridge was shaking
Jimmy Ray broke off the switch key
trying to start the car
with Bonnie Sue screaming in his ear
that it was God's punishment
for his wanting to go too far
and how it was really a sin to fool around
but Jimmy Ray, still thinking about that movie,
yelled out that he was going to run.

Without so much as a look back
he ran those four miles to town
Bonnie Sue shouting after him
above that train wreck
until she gave out of breath.
She was cursing him and squalling

when her daddy picked her up
over by the J.P. Stevens plant
but before getting in with him
she took off Jimmy Ray's class ring
and slung it far out into the woods.
He never did find it.

Moonlight Bridge: The bridge is located east of Calhoun Falls, SC, near State Highway 72 and was the scene of a derailment on April 11, 1975, in which 42 cars and 3 engines of the Seaboard Coastline Railroad jumped the tracks of the main line enroute from Hamlet, NC to Birmingham, AL. The 143 car freight train had departed earlier from Abbeville, SC. See: *The Calhoun Falls News,* 4-17-1975, p. 1.

Dr. Love's Last Flight

Standing there under a head-high ceiling
with wet mist bursting on his face
and Bentley's field socked-in by fog
he should have shrugged it off
and packed it in and gone back home
under those cool Sunday morning covers
and forgotten about making it to the Fliers Club
to show off that new plane
but something primal in him
turned off the switch of caution
and moved him through those stages
bound to make the dangerous risk acceptable
so that he opened up the throttle
and flew off down the runway blind
water beading like jewels on the windshield
and lifted out of the limp broom sage
to become a smudge against the sky.

Climbing to break through the underside
of warm and slippery milky pearl
pulsing like the suction cups
of a living thing against the windows
he sickened with the fright of hanging there
encapsulated by thick stifling premonitions
and as blind as Jonah in the belly
feeling nothing in a turn
to indicate the craft had moved
or leveled with the pressure of his hand.
Too panicked for the instruments
and praying from some suspended spot
just four miles out in the gray loneliness

he eased into a gentle glide
expecting to be spit out and reclaimed
upon a field or stretch of road
convinced that he could find a place
until the trees rushed up too late
and reached inside his shallow hopes
to drown him in a sheet of flame.

Dr. Love's Last Flight: On Sunday, April 29, 1951, Dr. C.H. Love, Jr., physician in Calhoun Falls, SC, was killed when his two-passenger Cessna 140 crashed in heavy fog shortly after 6:00 a.m., a few minutes after his take-off from Bentley's Field in Calhoun Falls. The scene of the crash was not discovered until the next morning and was 5 or 6 miles east near Sharon Church. Love had planned to pick up a friend in Abbeville and fly to the Fliers Breakfast Club in Newberry, SC. He had been flying for only 30 days and had owned the plane he flew for only three or four days. See: *The Calhoun Falls Times,* 5-4-1951, p. 1.

A Side-Trip Through Purgatory

If there are left among you
a few who have walked and known
the pleasures of unpaved roads
and who have seen the jasmine flower
trail down the side of a worn red bank
and smelled black pouting muscadines
hanging like jewels from vine-tired limbs
and felt the chill of a haint's breath
then some small sliver of creation
is briefly rescued and redeemed
and no hell-bound critic can complain
that it has been for nothing.

It is not by fate or circumstance
that those who strive are placed
in matching grooves of purpose
but by touching the old ripe moments
which hang suspended long enough
to be as real as the wagon ruts
that a small bare foot could fit in
and as soft as the powdered dust
in which it made a perfect track
for the man in the moon to watch
as he rose high and smiling
above flushed farm-cherished years.

In the drift of endless recent scenes
these moments press against the flesh
like sacred beads tightly-held
leaving warm indentions of innocence
which hold their pattern long enough
to grace each deep-seated yearning
with modest farm-fled expiations
and to become the righteous contents
of the effervescent dream
from which all truly wish to live
and finally wait to die
in the winnowing of their years.

Diamond Springs

The people are gone who laughed and dallied here
and allowed the simple world they knew
to slide quickly down time's banister
and into an age of complexity
taking with it feather beds and chamber pots
and rose water smells and cuspidors
and all the familiarities that got packed out
with the leather-bound trunks and grain sacks
on the last groaning wagon load
to straddle the hard-baked ruts
and turn its back on passing elegance
with the flick of a mule's ear.

The little pools of gaiety have all dried
under her tired and sagging double porches
with their bucked-up weathered floor boards
and silence stalks her forty vacant rooms
whose only recent guests include the owl
perched high in the shattered dormers
and dirt daubers reworking the entire third story
and the persistent yellow-hammering for admission
done against the shaded eaves on the back side
where blown-down veteran oaks
lie sprawled about like gypsies camped
and privet has over-grown and over-run
the slender pleading arms of the crepe myrtles.

Early leaves float on the mineral spring
clouded with the tea from broken limbs
its lips beaded with cracked glass jugs
that held the once-renowned elixir
favored above decantered wines and brandies
on the doilies in the foyers
and glistening like a medicine

in the glasses on the table
quaffed down by throngs and multitudes
who sought the proof and reassurance
as they waited out their lives
that it would gain them health and vigor.

Left to play the last time-honored hostess
to countless ebbing days and sinking nights
this vestige of false and groundless hope
has lived out her gilded stint
to stand diminished and abandoned
against the stark wooded back-drops
of a distant life and time
like a bitter aging woman
straining from a stair to catch
one last fleeting glimpse of interest
before returning to her former poise
and wishing for a merciful deliverance
by wind or flood or fire.

Diamond Springs: This old resort hotel, built five miles west of the town of Lowndesville, SC, on the Savannah River, began in 1837 with the development of a mineral springs by the Abbeville Mineral Springs Company. It was known and frequented by invalids seeking health cures, vacationers, and pleasure-seekers. Following the Civil War, its attraction declined. It was abandoned in the first quarter of the 20th century and burned in 1930 as a result of a woods fire. See: H.A. Carlisle, *History of Lowndesville, SC,* pp. 146-147.

Shadow Man

I am a shadow man
who casts himself against the grays of night
and passes through fleeting affections
like the unremembered contents of dreams
or the words of a table grace
that touch the clasp of a memory.

Entering the privacy of a moment
like a priest in a sickroom
I dispense ancient promises
into hushed and muted stillness
and I disrupt the sing-song litanies
of days and evenings
with subtle interventions
which ricochet off the senses
and embed themselves in the intuitions
of the heart.

On average days
I must digress into a transparency
of names and faces
no one remembers
while the gist of who I am
is tucked in the folds of consciousness
to await its resurrection
in those who will know me

A shadow man
identifiable but largely undisclosed
with powers to grant
the standard secret wishes
like some old genie in a bottle
whose form and substance are
for the world a vapor
but for you the purveyor of dreams.

Uncle Lean

Endings come so quickly
though his rocked on too long
and was still at a respectable distance
when he retired from police work in DC
and hauled the old leather-buckled trunk back South
and turned up at his sister's
who had held on to the home place
and just stood there in her yard
drinking it all in with his eyes
like an old exiled prince
come home to turn back all the pages
and remember the ones with gilded edges.

My bare feet followed his blue pin-striped stride
stepping in an impeccable shadow
of the derby and starched cuffs
on that day of special grace
fingers touching more than once
the black cane with the cut glass knob
that glittered when he pointed it
toward the old trunk-drilled pecan trees
he had planted in his youth
and gleamed along the streets of Calhoun Falls
when he stretched it like a scepter
where a mile of red oaks he set out
had been taken when the highway widened
except the one he patted lovingly
by the rusted grease rack
at the Lone Oak Service Station.

It should have ended there
with the kindness of a stroke
regaling before the bench Negroes
on the corner at the Red Dot Grocery
teeming with Homeric exhortations

or surprised by a massive coronary
while enlarging upon ordinary events
and soaking in the spilled wonder of a child
but it dragged on as some do
to a time long past reasonable suffrage
and a day of tiniest proportion
viewed through an inverted telescope
my adolescence bending over him
like a budding Hamlet stammering out his lines
there in the Veteran's Hospital in Augusta
where he lay strapped to a board
head shaven and strait-jacketed
eyes squeezed tight and face pinched
like some worm brought from slippery darkness
into a shrinking embarrassment of light
ending only when a curtain slapped
the gawking face of innocence.

Uncle Lean: Cleo Tucker (1892 - 1964) grew up in the town of Calhoun Falls, SC, and spent nearly twenty years of his early adulthood away from home. He relocated in Greenville, SC, in 1957, where he lived until his death. He died in the Veteran's Hospital in Augusta, GA. The poem reflects a visit made to him shortly before his death while he was hospitalized there.

Reversion

In these fledgling months
when bee and early flower are confused
by a thick frozen breath
blown over the waiting fields
and ice is found in the lining
of earth's outer garments
and birds who left the raucous flocks
to separate themselves by twos
gather back along the empty wires
all that is left for living things
who would survive these fusillades
is to find some scant shelter
safe from the killing doubts
and to begin to peck and feed
on that coarser knowledge
that all kept promises are hard
in a land where tombstones and jonquils
both face east.

Storm Warning

The day Cleet Hudlow got himself a motorcycle
and was burning up the pavement with it
out on the Peach Orchard Road
he noticed clouds off to the east
and figuring to outrun them
cut it wide open and headed in
and had just topped the hill by the shed
white streamers popping in the handle-bar grips
when his front wheel hit some culls
some nit-brain had thrown in the road
and put him into a sideways skid
that forced him to jump for the ditch
while his bike clattered down the pavement
like ice slung out of a car window.

Cleet got up still and trembling
his face white with shock
and the back of his black cycle jacket
covered with rotten pulp and peach pits
and moved his skint bike to the side
where he tried to get it kick-started.
He was just catching his wind
when a jagged yellow pitchfork
cut through the ozone and fused itself
to a post in the orchard fence
leaving the top two strands of wire
glowing like the eye of a burner
and tumbling Cleet into the stark realities
of that same peach-filled ditch
with bees and blow-flies and rotten fruit
conspiring against that smug image of himself
worn moments earlier like a badge
but dissipated by the crude reminders
from a world he hoped to rise above.

Dazzled by the naked streak of light
dry-mouthed half-dead and weightless
he rose like a Lazarus in black leather
and was standing up in the ditch
brushing off his smelly jacket sleeves
when another bolt rolled him
breathing down his turned-up collar
like hot fumes from the mouth of hell
Cleet reduced to groveling and terrified
when Old Man Tred Epps who owned the shed
saw him drowning in the rain that followed
and gave himself a good drenching
to bring him safe under the hammering tin
where he was propped on a crate
and asked why he had no better sense
Tred offering him a slice of life he had peeled
from a faulty one not fit to sell
and Cleet biting into its slippery flesh
while he fumbled for an answer.

A Word In Private

Wrapped in a shroud of quiet
the morning fog encroaches
upon the rights of all
who entertain horizons
bringing nearer to the eye
long-fled apparitions
gone unnoticed in the bid
for all that is removed
and distant.

In muted contemplations
on this veiled and clouded road
where headlamps float about
like disconnected souls
and a sense of direction
serves no immediate purpose
the thought of home
hangs like an incandescent flare
on the mist
promising to burn through
to the darkness of the barn
and touch the tired child
who fell asleep among the apples.

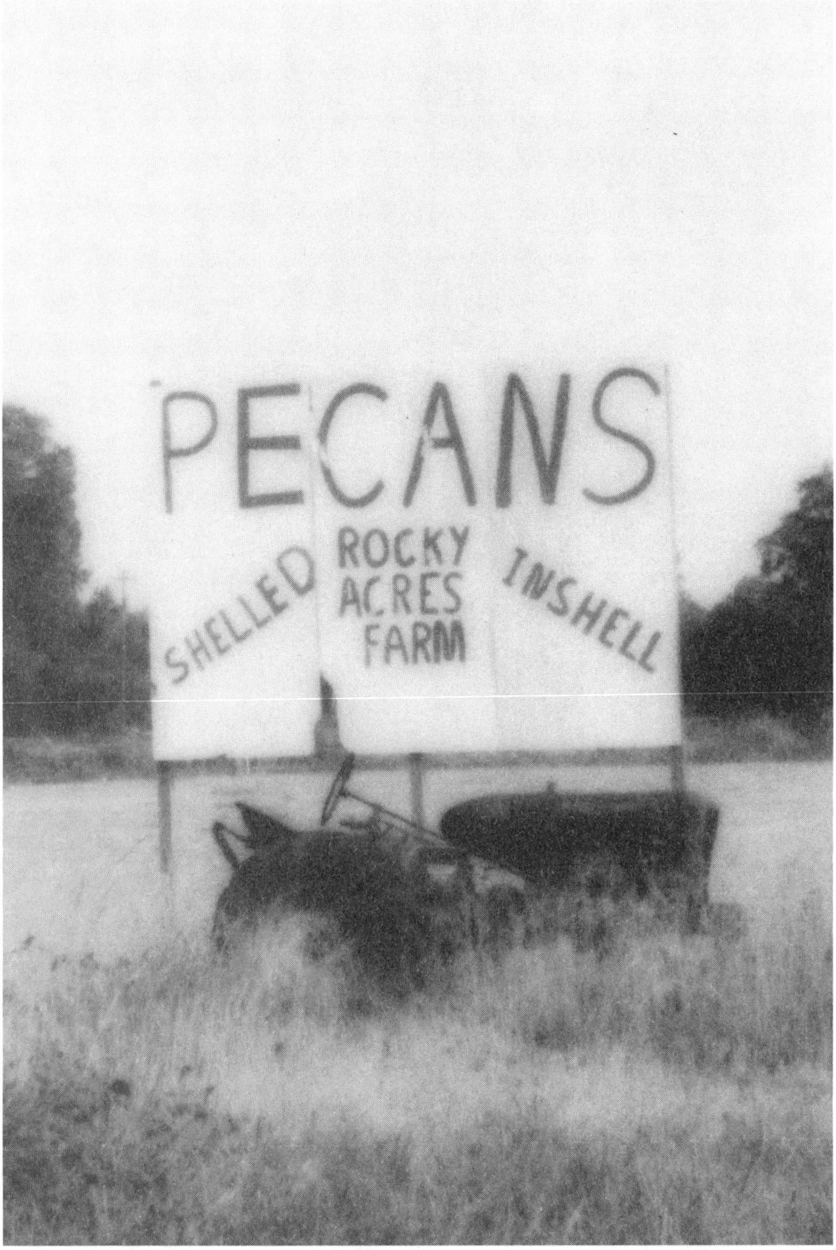
PECANS
SHELLED
ROCKY
ACRES
FARM
INSHELL

Latimer Curve

Sammy got his
in that elongated split-second
when his eyes left the road
to look at those gravestones
out the window on the left-hand side
as they stood stark and irresistible
drawing his head around like a magnet
and tugging on that morbid fascination in him
for the dead and buried.

The instant he jerked back on the wheel
he realized the over-compensation
and the righted world left him
his '55 Fairlane flipping twice
finally to come to rest
on its crushed egg-shell top
wheels still spinning above the broom-sage
and glass scattered like diamonds on the ground
and Sammy snapped and slammed
and tossed out from it
like a lost ball in the high weeds.

The patrolman doing the measuring
and making the notations
never could figure out what got into Sammy
finding no skid marks at the scene
and knowing he had to be going over 75
to be slung that far.
Anybody who had driven it one time
knew about that curve
and his being asleep at the wheel
wasn't likely at ten o'clock in the morning.

It never was surmised or determined
just what the cause was
but Sammy finally got his
about three weeks later.
It was a fine white one
with his name on it
and it stood out a little from the others
in the new part of the cemetery
where it could face toward the road
and be seen first
out the windows on the left-hand side.

Girl Of Glass

In the changing window embroidery
of this endless rain
the light that catches
in these delicate prisms
turns only for an instant
giving an illusion of beauty
in the gray shimmering beads
before bleeding off the panes
like tears from the face
of the one who is watching
their overlay on her reflection
with eyes dark and glistening
that do not see the wet
empty streets of the night
or the tide that chokes the gutters
and belches down the spouts
yet who senses in her stare
a melancholy spot that marks
the confluence of emotions
where the stream of righteousness
passes quickly under the bridge
of pain.

The Blue Hole Gang

On a night like no other
with the river washed in golden mists
of a rising moon
and the path through the woods lit
all the way to that place
where boys could go back and be
themselves again
five of them walked it
pulling tree limbs out of the way
and peeling back all the layers
separating them from the fragile intimacies
of who they were.

All it took was a seine and a skillet
some corn meal and a little grease
and a pint apiece of what could be had
to get body and soul together
for all those juvenile aspirations
dry-laundered for over forty years
to pick up right where they left off
and reconnect the wandering hopes
burning for the longest
in their hollow sunken eyes.

The Hole had shrunk down
like their necks and faces
in the over-large shirt collars
but there was enough spring water
with the leaves and trash dipped out
to make their teeth ache
and to satisfy once more
the alcoholic burn left in their throats
and firelight enough
to make the place respectable.

The daring and swearing moved with the owls
down to the river's burnished bank
and Dice waded out and anchored down the seine
until he gave out of breath
while Simp worked the sandy shallows
and made his haul
and soon the wood smoke and memories
were hanging out there at the Hole
to be winked at and fondled
like those yellow-bellied mudcats
hot and irresistible on the fingers
and blistering on the palate going down.
God! Old Acey could still cook'em
as fast as the others could skin'em
and bread'em down!

After a dozen rounds of drinks
and hand-rolled smokes were put to bed
it was a night to talk out desperate times
and recollect the rhymes and sayings
of the absent dead
whose smiles and sins came back
and glowed awhile in the dying coals
before the wind laid.
There was Shorty with the crinkled eyes
back in the thirties
compelled by thirst to squeeze Jamaica Ginger
through loaf-bread in the prohibition years
until he and Lefty got the Jakes
when the stuff got mixed with stock dip
in that Atlanta tanker car . . .
and there was old Jim Roy
who could have made a preacher
except for his affection for the boys
out at the Hole
who scotched him with a brace or two
on the evenings he would hold forth.
Old Jim Roy blew his finger off
fooling with a pocket pistol
after a losing streak with cards
and later blew out his own brains . . .

and then there was Eugene with the mean streak
and Pearl with the bad eye
and old Cuz who froze to death
right out there under the stars
and was carried out stiff as they come
by some of the others . . .
all gone now
blown off like leaves whispering
on a bone-chilling night.

Finishing it out and dozing for awhile
someone got up later
and added on a limb or two
and watched the sparks shoot up
riding a trail of smoke
on a thread of darkness
just like a parting soul would.
And the night air filled with sour breaths
and the broken snores
of those who lay dew-beaded
lost in a grateful oblivion
which granted them some small hedge
against the morning.

The Blue Hole Gang: The Blue Hole was a place on the Savannah River, not far
from the town of Calhoun Falls, SC, where a number of persons regularly drank,
gambled and congregated. In time, these persons became known as the "bay-rum
boys" and were considered alcoholics. Over the years they aged and faded from
view. There are many stories of events that happened at the Blue Hole, a spring
now under the waters of the Richard B. Russell Lake.

Absolution

Familiar stars have changed position
and the chill is heavier on this night
as if some great conspiracy
among the hanging planets
has provoked from distant darkness
an adolescent mood-swing
setting nature's modest passions
in an uproar.

Tomorrow the great eye
of the sky will open
red-rimmed and bleary
from moon-lit frolic
and conduct its sober business
of bringing warmth and light
amid clean clearing winds
and slight but stinging frosts.

In the gold and glistening woods
new autumn fires will burn
scorching the sweet gums and tinting
the hickory with licking flames
as squirrels race around the trunks
chiding themselves to exhaustion
and bucks in rut
on the beech-leaf carpet
stamp and snort and drip with musk.

The molten fire will creep
into every cold abstraction
reaching in and never out
to darkened shapes of glass and steel
and to each four-walled room
under a pale fluorescent ceiling
always pointing in not out
as this mystery penetrates
the continence of tired flesh
enough to cough a fax machine to life
and will a matrix print-out
of a buckeye and a poplar leaf.

Brother Johnson

Every town has got one
and Sparta is no different
entrusting its public image for all times
unwittingly to the likes of one
who never tires at playing the fool
or becoming the unofficial greeter
to an endless train of passersby
who size up all there is to know
according to his countenance.

Standing like a favored saint
dispensing blessings with his gestures
or walking about the streets
with an owner's sense of pride
at every car he smiles and tips his hat
eyes penetrating the tinted panes
and boring into blank impassive stares
until they touch a soft spot
with a twinge of recognition
that creates linkage soul to soul.

Those who know the truth
and pass off his uniqueness
as the bud and bloom of an affliction
stemming from a complicated birth
and shake their heads in sadness
have missed the greater truth
that pollinates these little towns
and sterile courthouse squares
and narrow stifling streets
with the grist of angels silver-shod.

Wintering

After the harshness has run its course
and skies are purged of wind and ice
those who have survived the season change
stand out under its blue emptiness
in bright checkered flannel shirts
and old broad-brimmed felt hats
exercising their freedom from fear
of all bed-fast infirmities
but rooted to a favorite spot
like old porch dogs in the sun.

If they move at all
it is to haunt old sheds and out-buildings
looking in rusting cans and buckets
with a cold and glittering curiosity
for things left and long forgotten
or to pick at a string in their clothes
and pull at it with their thoughts
until they yield or it breaks
and they can enjoy the shallow draught
of feeble fading men.

Worn down and smoothed on time's wheel
like the blades of out-dated implements
abandoned in dusty silk-webbed corners
they have been disgraced by uselessness
in the solitude of grim backrooms
and yet are sly when mimicking its traits
having satisfactorily and for one more year
cheated the death angel of his due
and tied him in a sack someplace
and left him to shift for himself.

Christmas In A Mill Town

Out of that dark black endless void
beyond the street light's yellow circle
the same shining color as the panther
on the dime-firecracker package
bottle-rockets, cherry bombs and sparklers
held just far enough from glowing cheeks
ignited every frost-trimmed Christmas Eve
and no one lost a thumb
or put another's eye out
though a dormant Roman candle ball
got up a boy's pants leg
and burned a dark blue hole.

After singing at the town tree
in the bend of the main drag
with a lump in every throat
the crowd thinned out and then reformed
when someone found Curly wadded in a ball
against the granite war monument
behind the blown-out luminaries
with his jaw sliced open
on a broken liquor bottle
and then got old Doc Ward
to sew him up by flashlight
without giving him anything.

The late night shouts and slamming doors
of a card-room second-shifter
broke through the dreamless sleep
that nestled in the drab houses
to proclaim his boys' Christmas stolen
from his own back porch
tumbling neighbors from their beds
to follow the police chief to a house

where he recovered tents and boots and belts
and other Army surplus goods
without warrant or arrest
to desecrate the night divine.

A killing in a cafe in Buck Nelly
which left one Negro dead
and a clinging family wet with grief
finished out that silent night
of violent nights
and bare feet hit the floor
and found the bulging sacks
of raisins, nuts and oranges
and whatever else was promised
so that all were lifted free
from what they were
to touch the softness of a moment
waiting there under the bubble lights
so warm, so real,
so out of place.

Last Rites

The way the last leaves
hold to the young red oaks
after the others have gone
only gives them cause
to chafe their ragged sorrow.

Not yet ready to detach themselves
and be blown about by elements
to far and alien places
they have defied the charge
to drop and mingle
with those that have been snatched away
and scattered to the winds.

From a heightened state of union
they have enjoyed the season
reluctant to break away
and lose their rightful place
but consigned to grovel far below
and own this severing.

In the greening
they are content to cling there
providing a semblance of protection
until the new growth
renders them useless
and unnecessary.

Indian Graves

We told him not to build it there
near those gray rock piles
hanging off that little ridge like carbuncles
on the sags of dried ancient skin
but he had the ditches dug
for the water line and septic tank
in one earth-jarring afternoon
waving off our light insinuations
with the recoil of a tent preacher
giving a hurried benediction.

On the evening of the first day
and every one that followed for a month
rain in torrents filled the ditches
and water stood all season
brim-full and teeming with snakes and frogs
that knotted on the wire mesh strainer
of the sump-pump like old root clogs
in a terra cotta drain
until the hired labor quit
and he had to rent his own machine.

When the first course of blocks was laid
against the pulled string that fall
a wind blew in before the mortar dried
uprooting red oaks on that one hill
and hurling them like javelins
into the wet foundation
scattering blocks and plans and batter-boards
back along smooth familiar routes
to their points of origin
in the ink wells of the imagination.

Two of the three who framed it in
before the first firm grip of winter
left the dank shadows of the house
to go in for nails and coffee
while the one whose hammer rang
and echoed in that lonely place
looked through sooty scrap-pile warmth
and beheld the spirits of the dead
rising with the vapors on the hill
like old fears coming for him.

He lost his cigarette as he fell
headlong over a gas can
but made it out to the highway
perspiration streaming through his clothes
and an ice-white stare in his eyes
that never once looked back to see
the oily smudge that grew and blinked
its red eye through the trees
like a favorite hound turned crazy
glowering from the porch.

The black rectangle smouldered for three days
despite a drenching cleansing rain
which splattered ashes in long rivulets
down into the mowing field
as stark and bare as the waning months
but all was hidden in the spring
by a towering stand of poke weed
interspersed among the skunk cabbage
its white plumes disregarded by the owner
who chose another spot.

Grist From Other Mills

I.
Similitudes

In anagogic moments
all of the classic themes
involuntarily repeat themselves
like whispered conversations
in a sanctuary
reciting the gist of Homer
and fragmentary lines of Aesop
laced with tidbits and droppings
running through the wisdom of Solomon
and every lead-lined casket abstract
buried in human consciousness
from parables to nursery rhymes
harkening back to once upon a time
when the world was crisp and new
and connecting each heroic episode
with who one is to be
in this endless chain of names and faces.

Those who would mediate these exchanges
must leave the secure provinces
deep within themselves
venturing as true knights errant
and pass into the sovereign territories
of a malevolent but legendary realm
where there are no shining cities
to refresh them as they forage there
and endure the waiting.

II.
Passage

I wait inside myself
daily
for an opening
in the fabric of time
to slip quietly through
to the Other Side.

Nerve endings are bunched
in readiness
gathered strength is poised
yet the borders are heavily patrolled
and telepathic word goes out .
there is no escaping
this place.

Breathing in this stale life
no longer at ease here
I long for grace enough
to find a wrinkle
in the transparent envelope
through which the tired unclean may pass
and bathe themselves in light.

III.
Gingko

Delicate survivor
whose rigid panels
shimmered in the winds of creation
when the sun glistened early
upon the rims of the world
and whose yellow fans
have moved in floating motions
above the slime of centuries

I have watched for such a moment
to touch the glory of your dying
and press your beauty
between these folds
preserving it
for times to come.

The ancients of my kind
stitched your thin discs
into a crude parchment
and left their poetry
as light as air
with gentle brush strokes.

One haiku
I will write here
as an offering to these memories
and in tribute:

Shining silver apricot
permitting me to touch
a lover's moon.

IV.
Dissolution

There are covenants
that have been swept away
like leaves in a cold rush
of winter wind
gone forever from the bough
and no one can be faulted
in their going.

For ever so long
they rattle and make their noise
but gradually lose definace
as they turn black and soft
and melt into the earth
to become as nothing
and for their memory
there will be no stone.

Benediction

Joy will come round again
like a migratory bird
or an old gypsy
with the canvas rolled up
on his wagon
to tent awhile with us.

And peace will return
like a long-absent friend
with whom we enjoyed
the sun-washed days
and it will be as though
the interim were a moment.

In the space between then and now
when all seems lost and disconnected
time will teach us
the preciousness
of that for which we wait
and like grass coming back
in the dead fields
our hope will live
to nourish us
until we die.

About the Author

Harold Lawrence grew up in a small mill town in South Carolina. He is a United Methodist pastor currently serving in Milledgeville, Georgia.